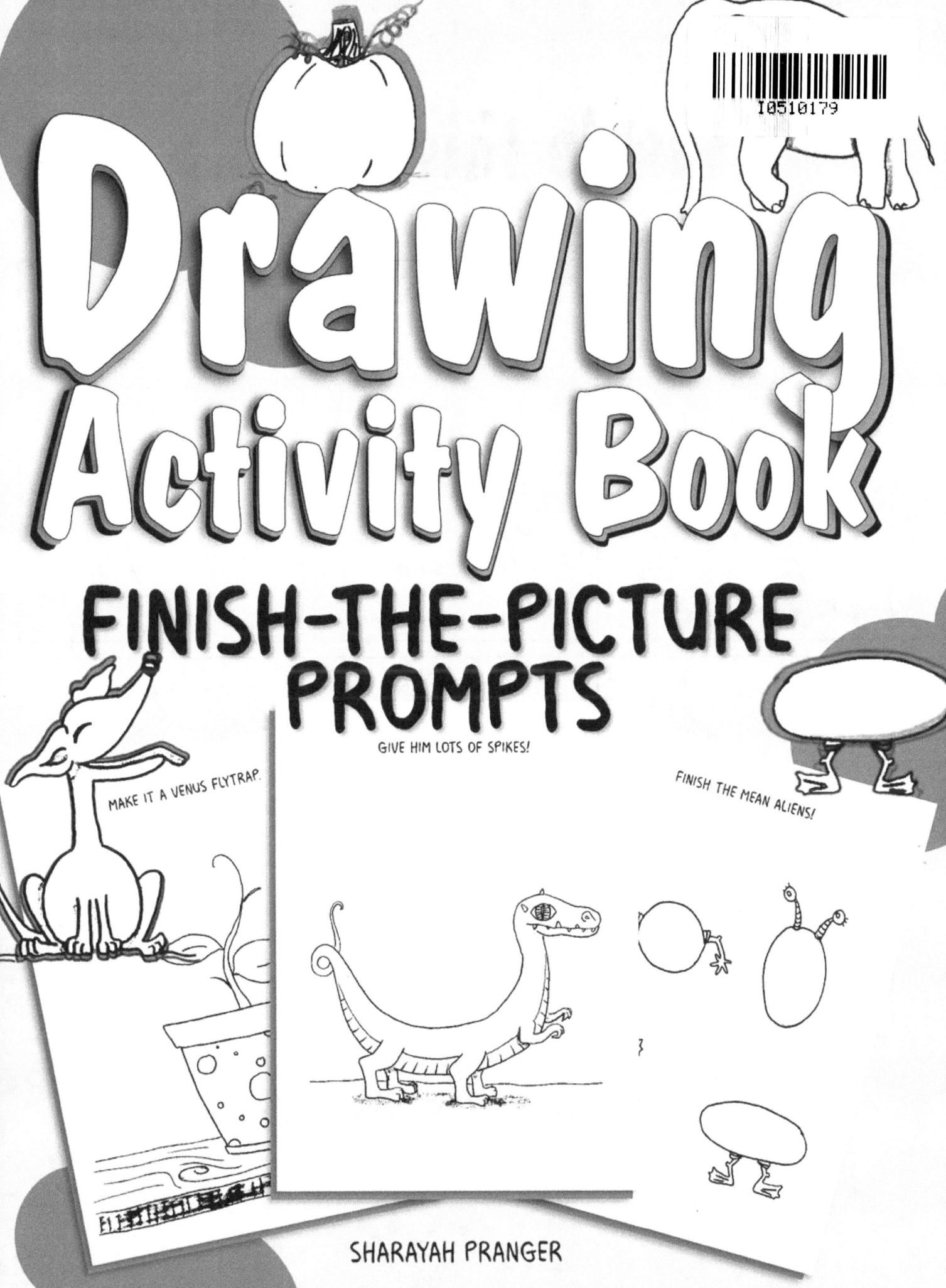

Drawing
Activity Book
FINISH-THE-PICTURE PROMPTS

MAKE IT A VENUS FLYTRAP.

GIVE HIM LOTS OF SPIKES!

FINISH THE MEAN ALIENS!

SHARAYAH PRANGER

Inside this book...

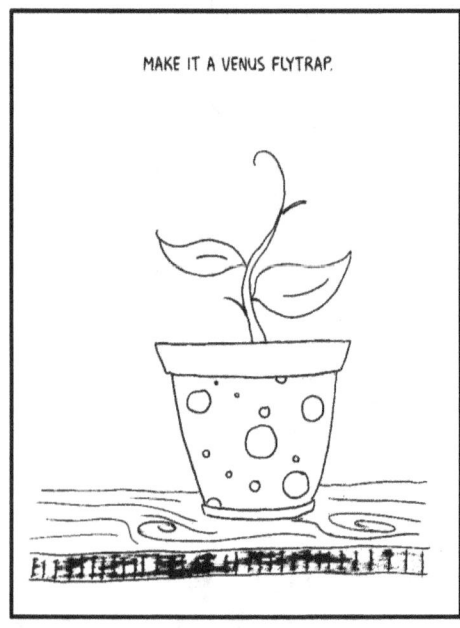

MAKE IT A VENUS FLYTRAP.

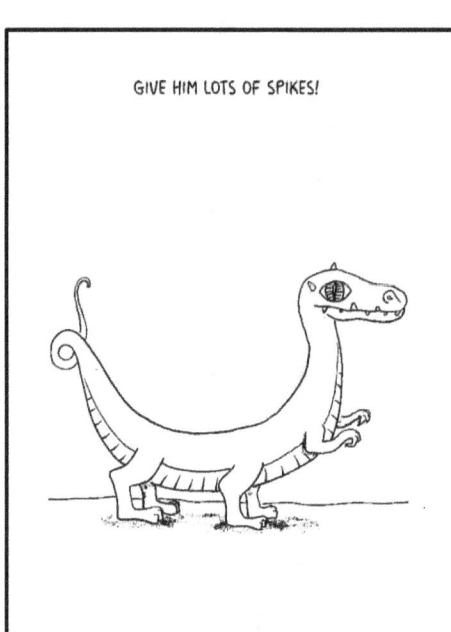

GIVE HIM LOTS OF SPIKES!

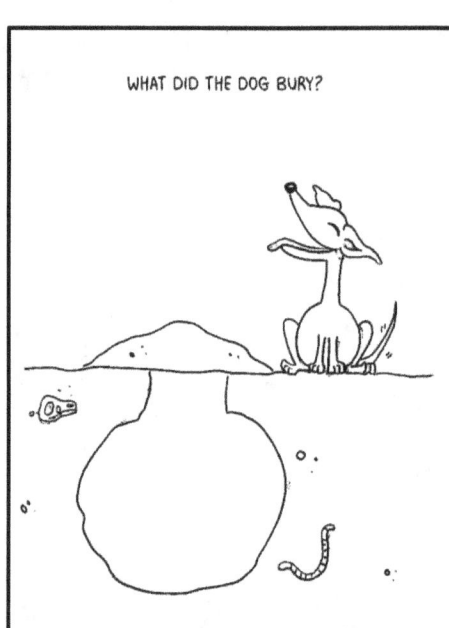

WHAT DID THE DOG BURY?

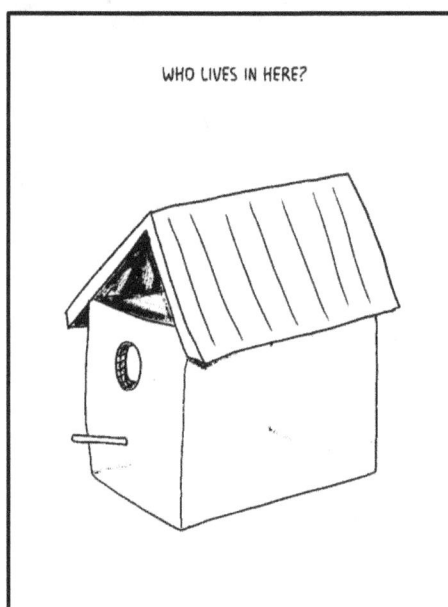

WHO LIVES IN HERE?

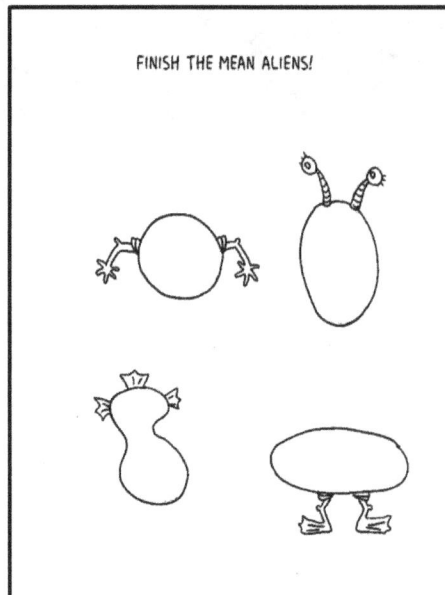

FINISH THE MEAN ALIENS!

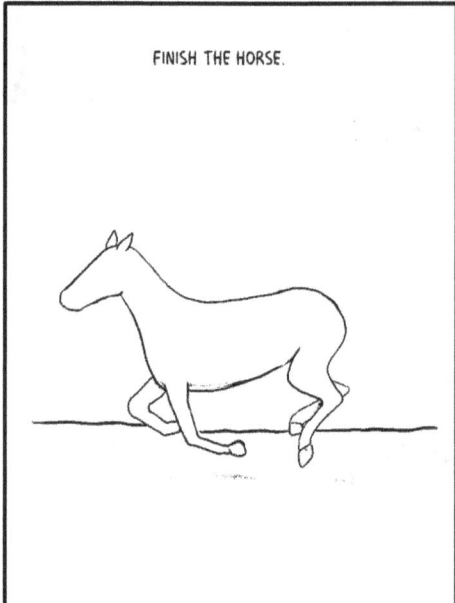

FINISH THE HORSE.

And much more!

GIVE HIM LOTS OF SPIKES!

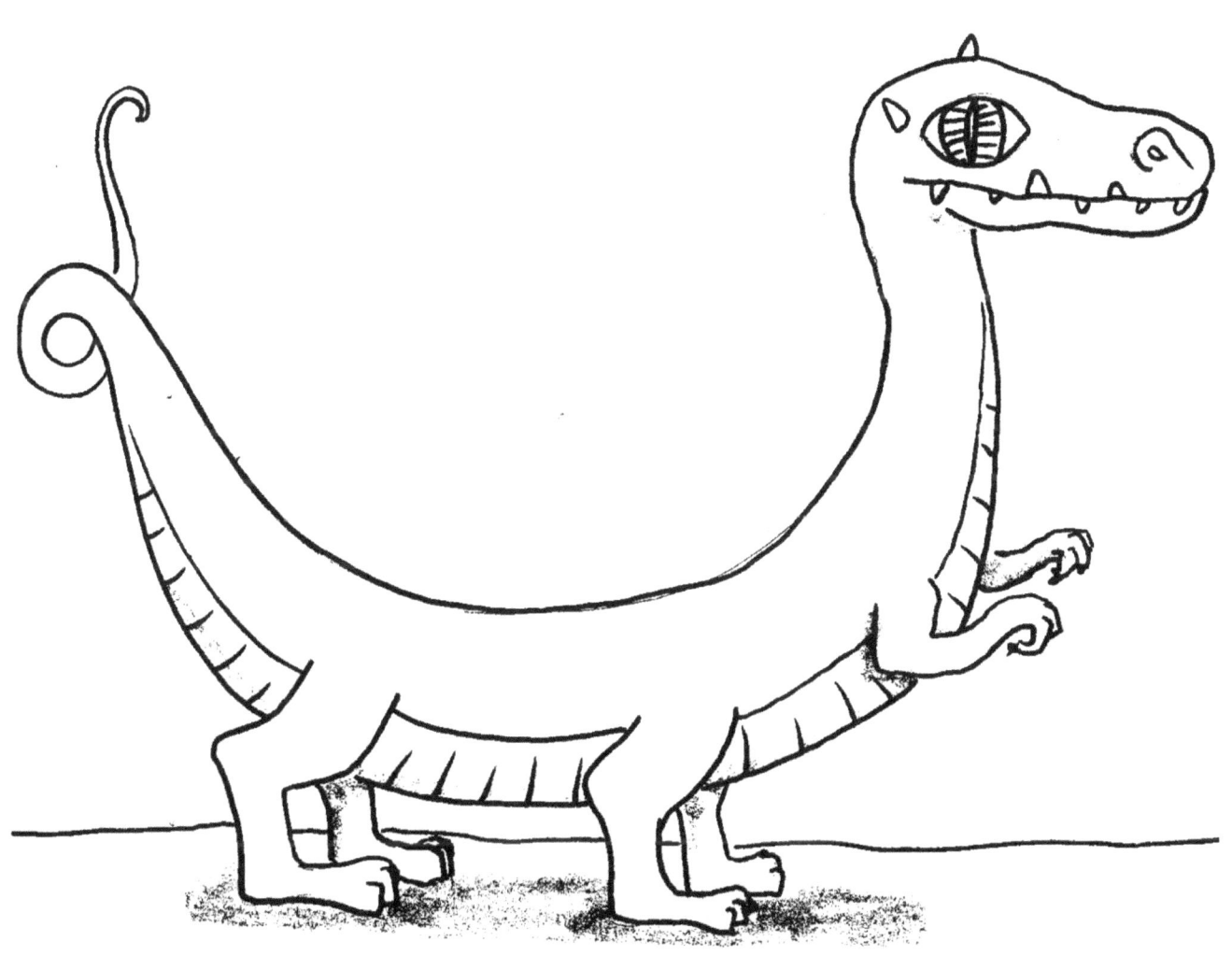

GIVE THIS PUMPKIN A SILLY FACE.

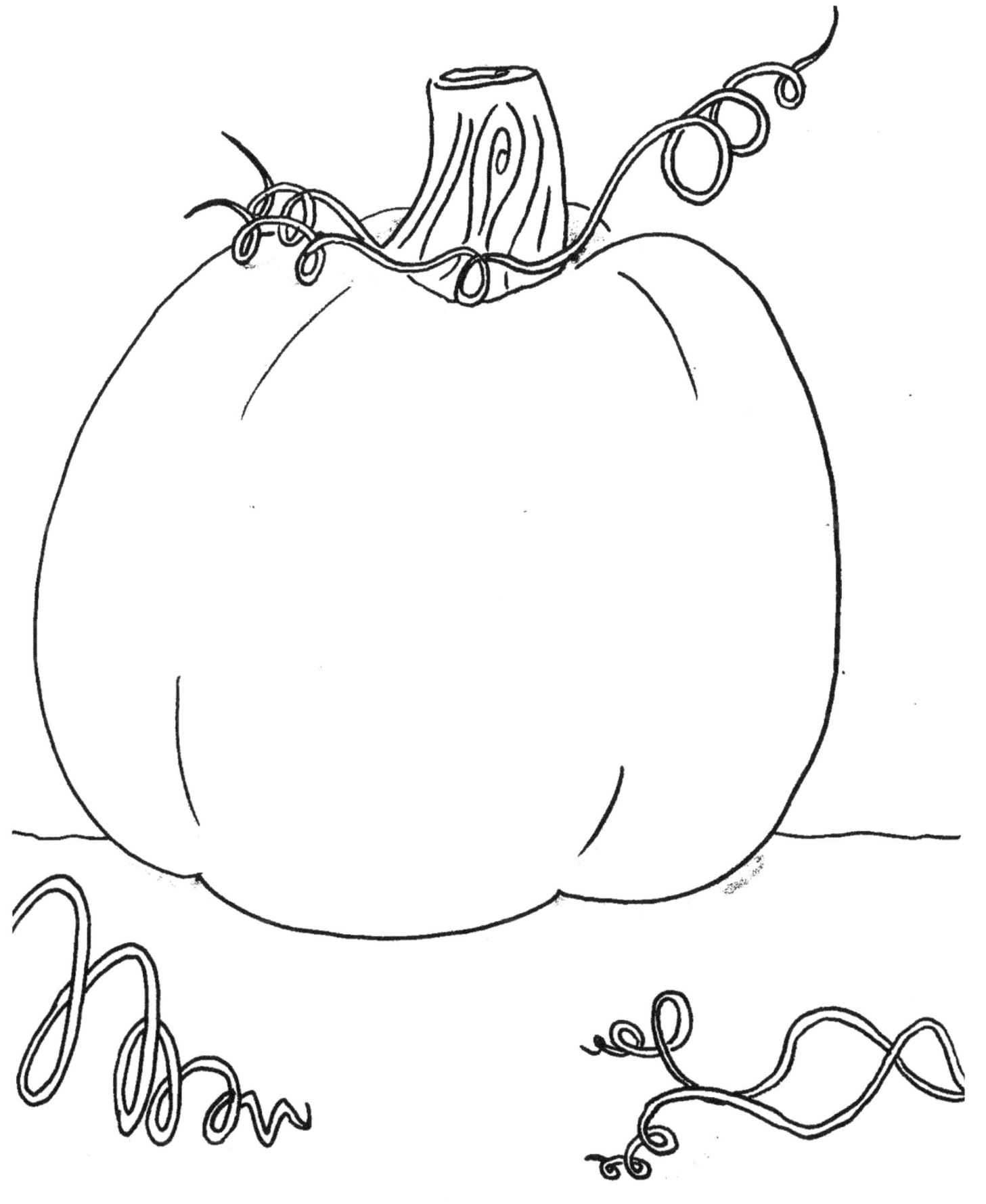

WHAT DID THE DOG BURY?

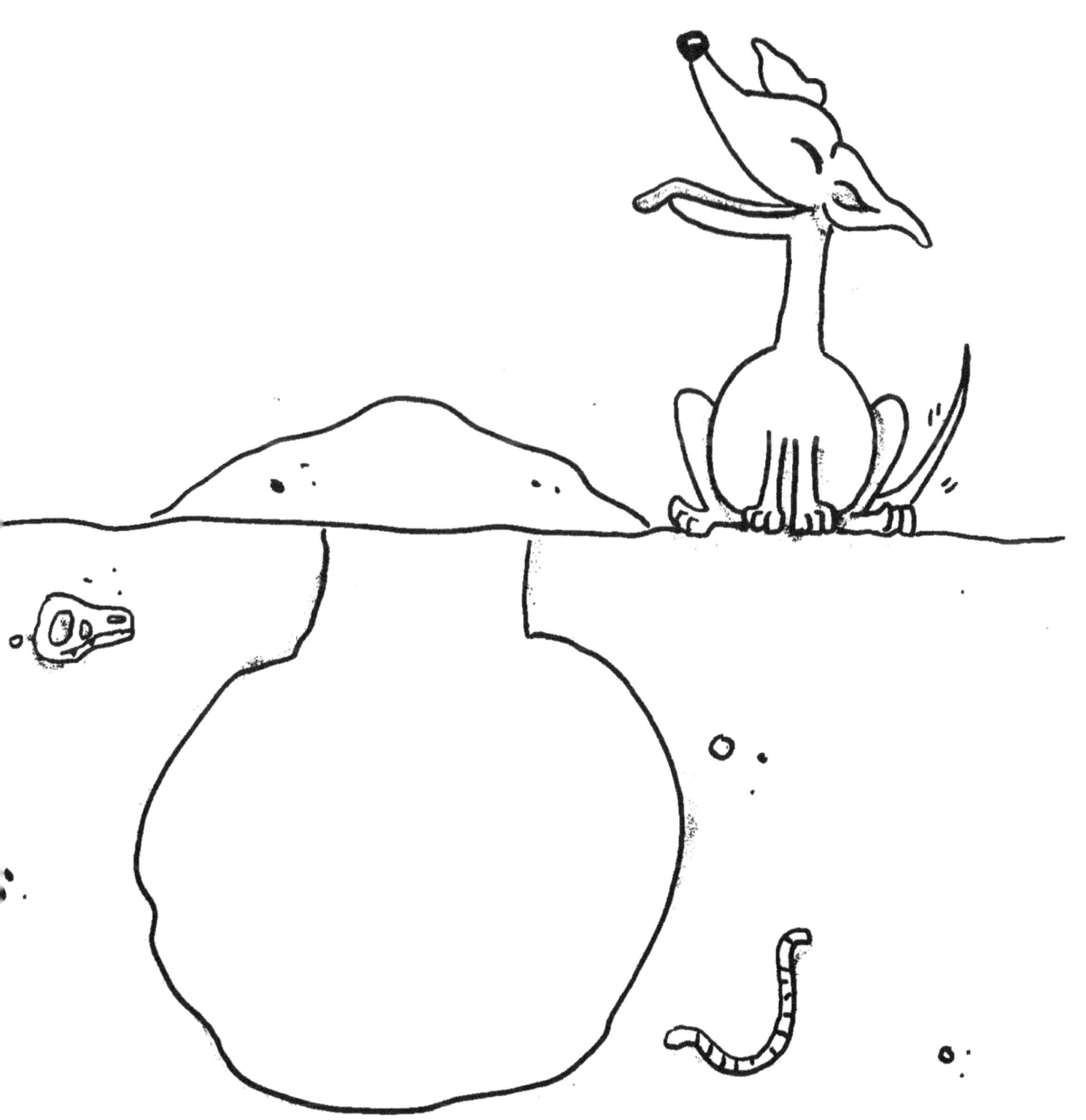

WHO LIVES IN HERE?

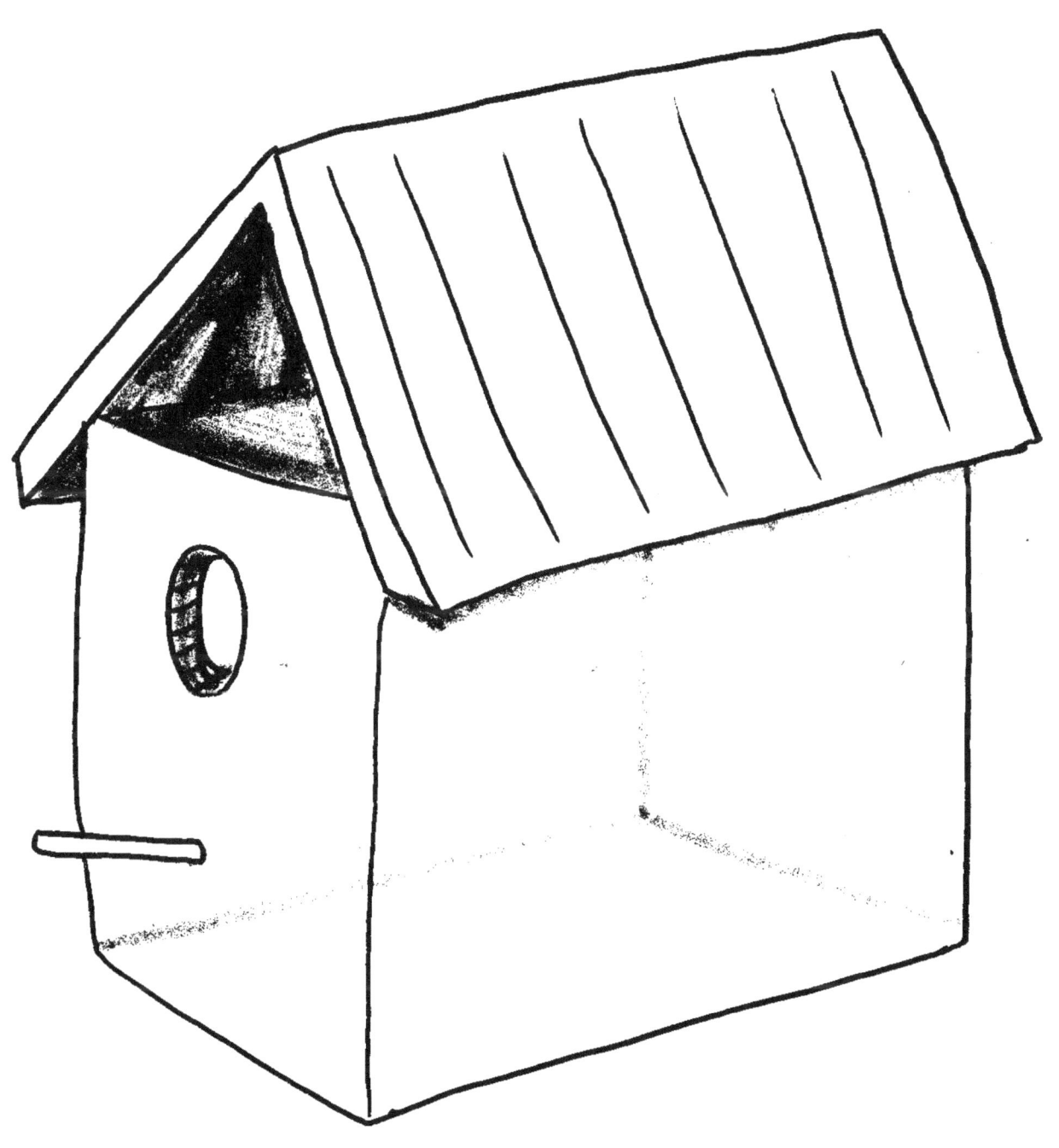

WHAT'S FOR DINNER?

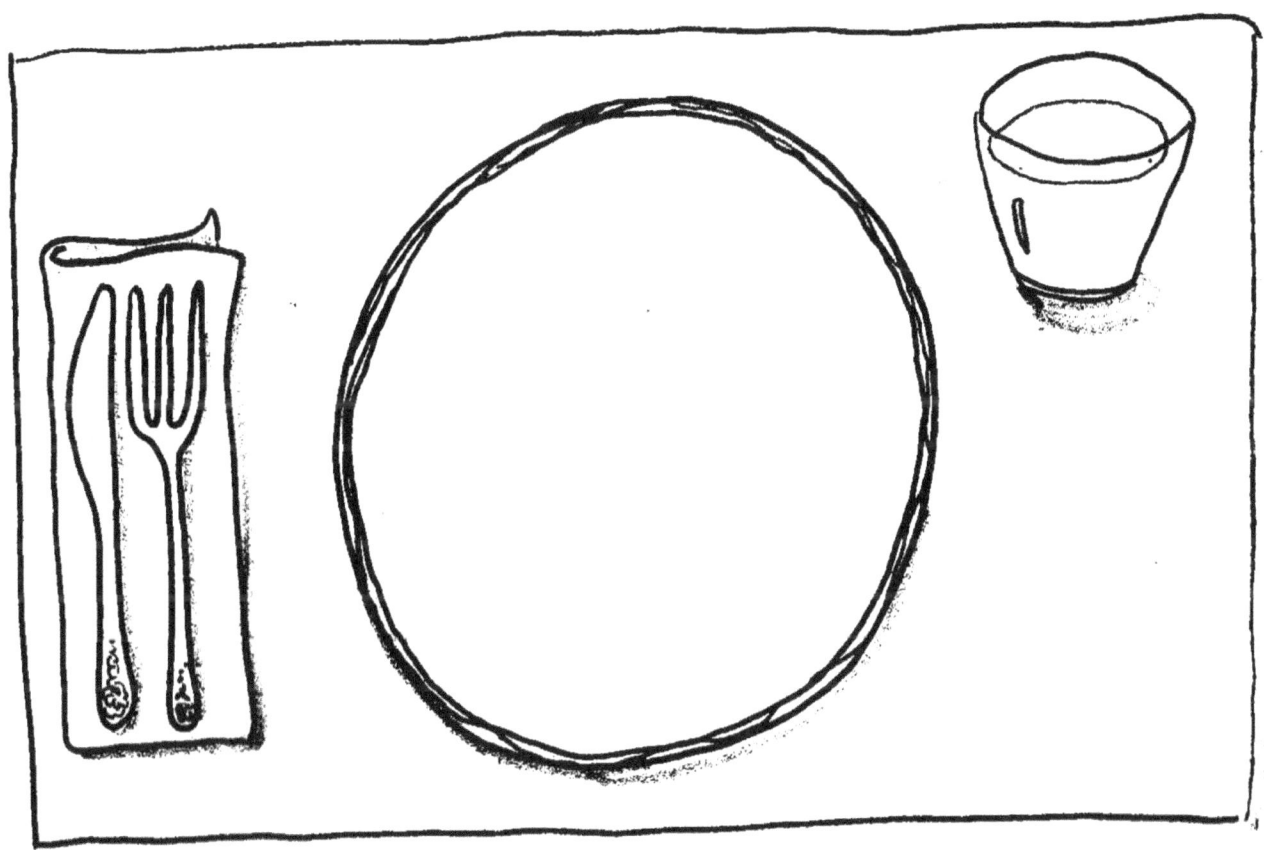

WHO LIVES IN HERE?

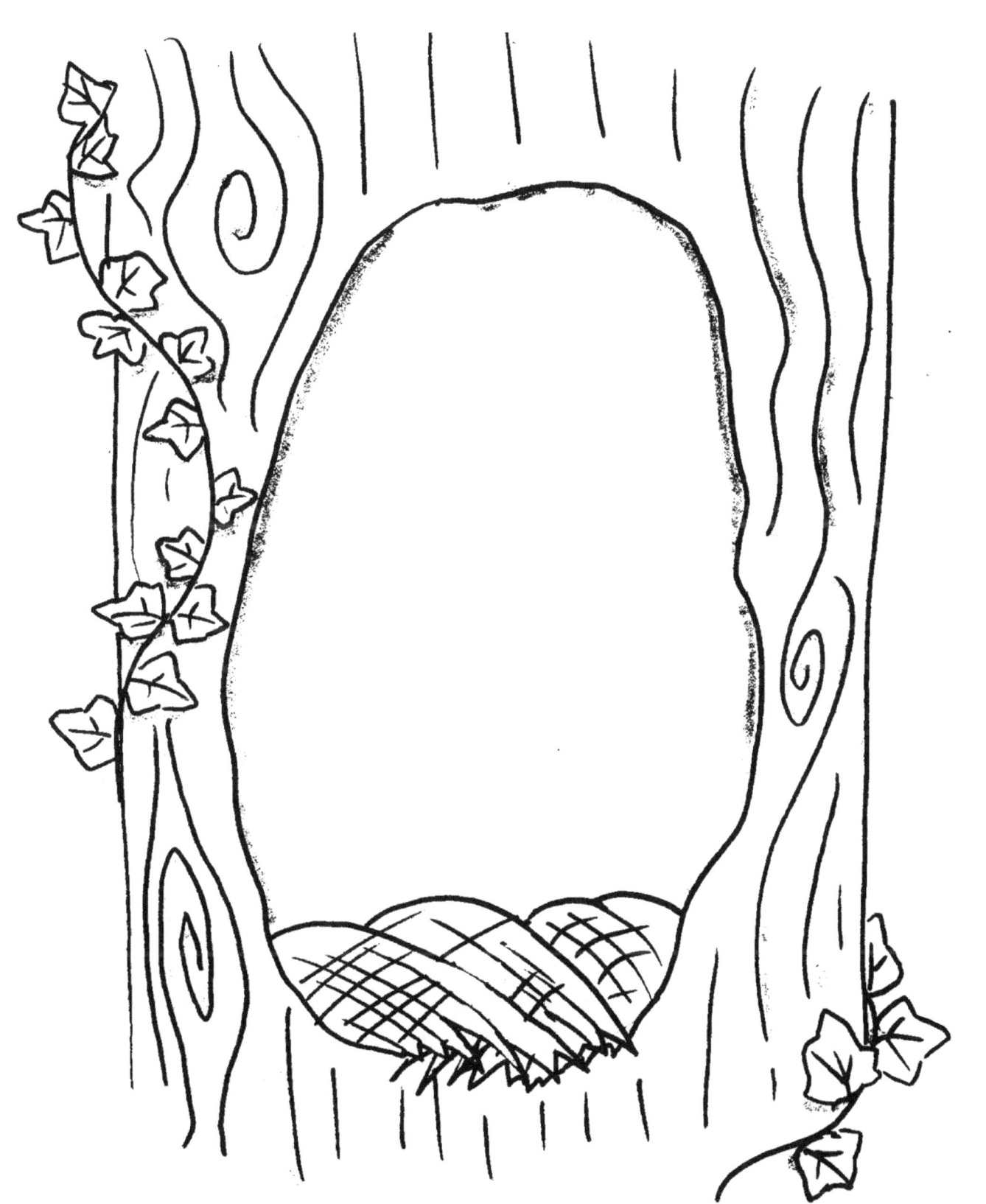

WHO LIVES IN HERE?

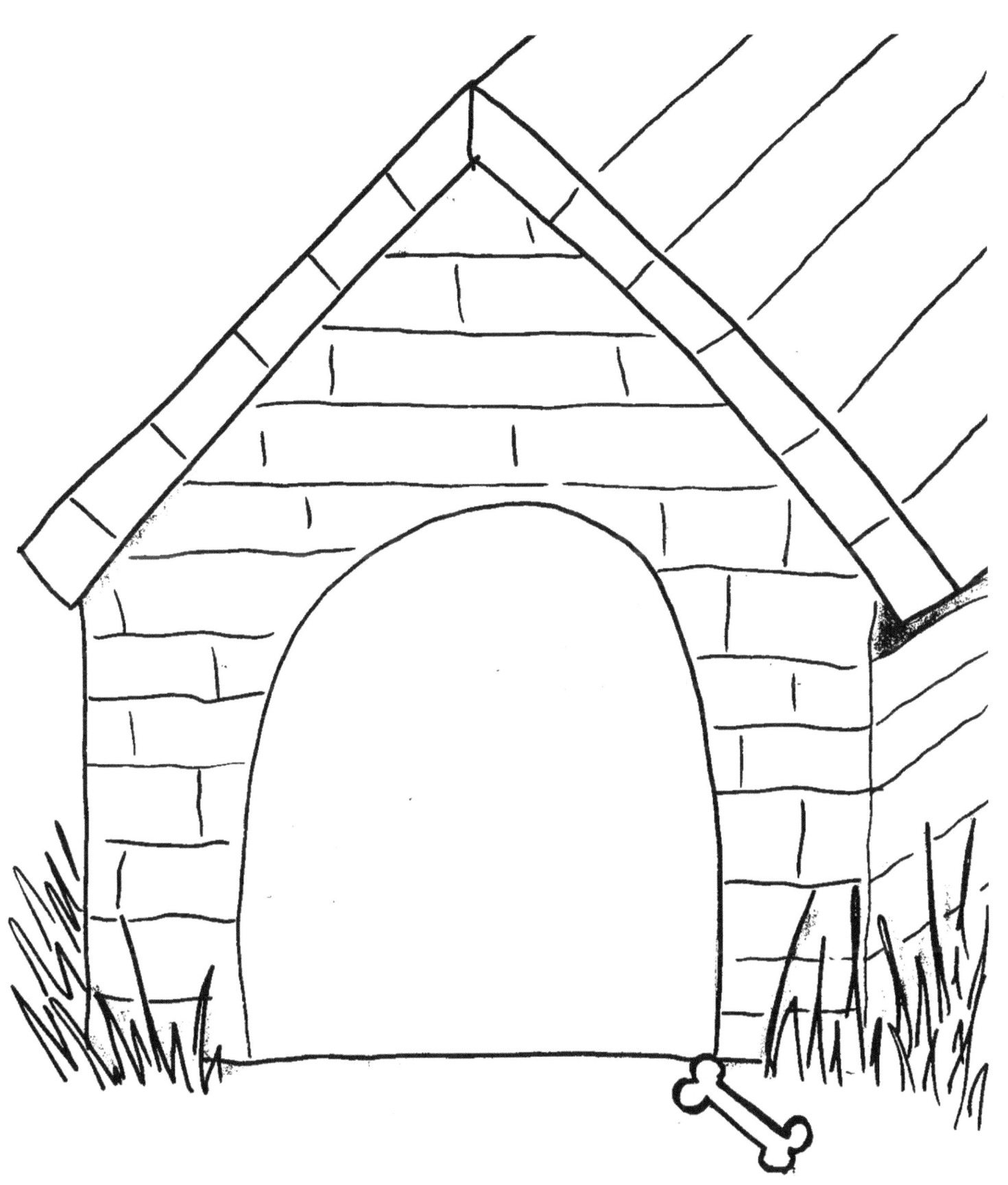

WHAT'S GROWING ON THIS PLANT?

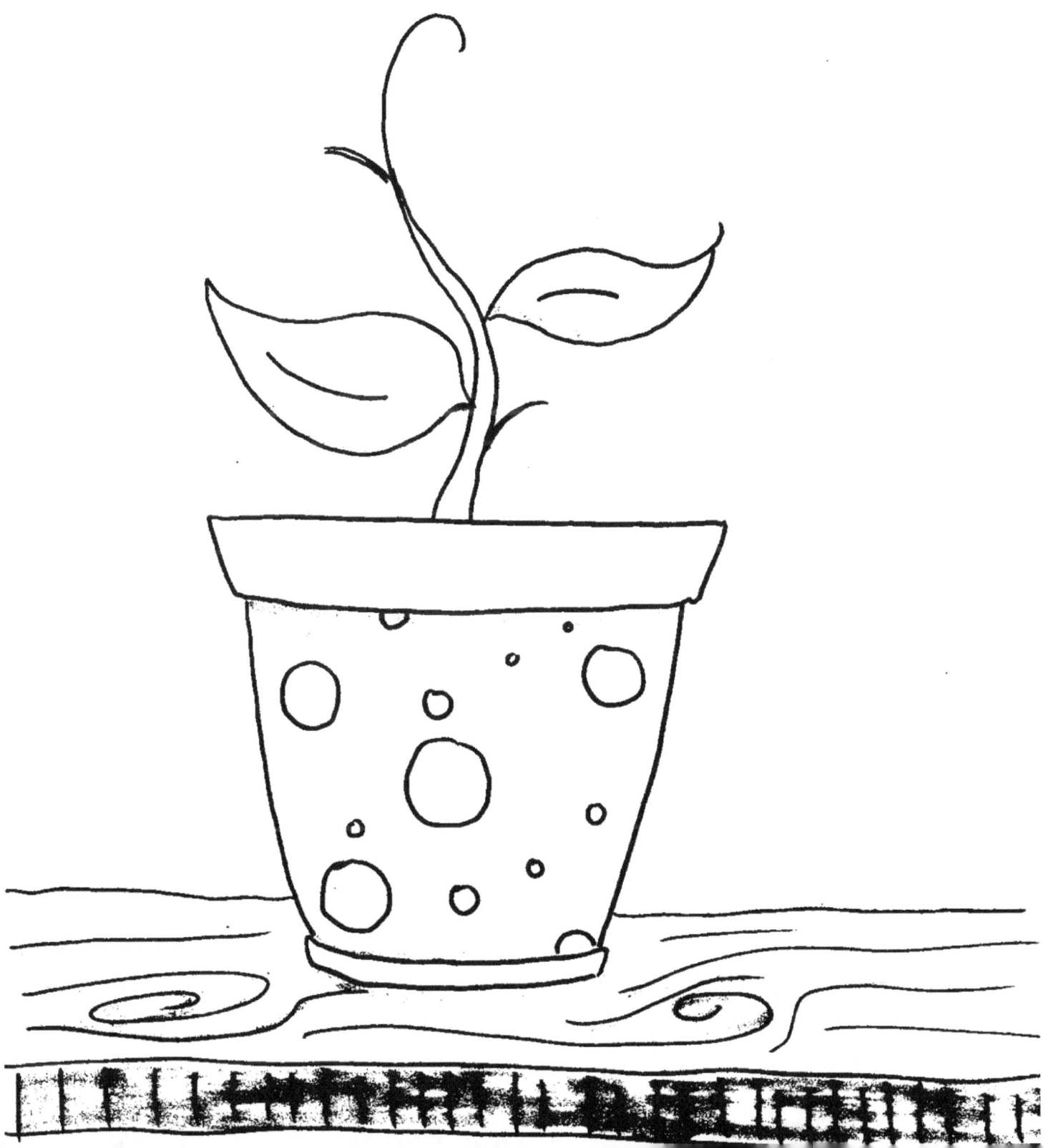

WHAT GOT CAUGHT IN THE WEB?

DECORATE SOME CHRISTMAS COOKIES!

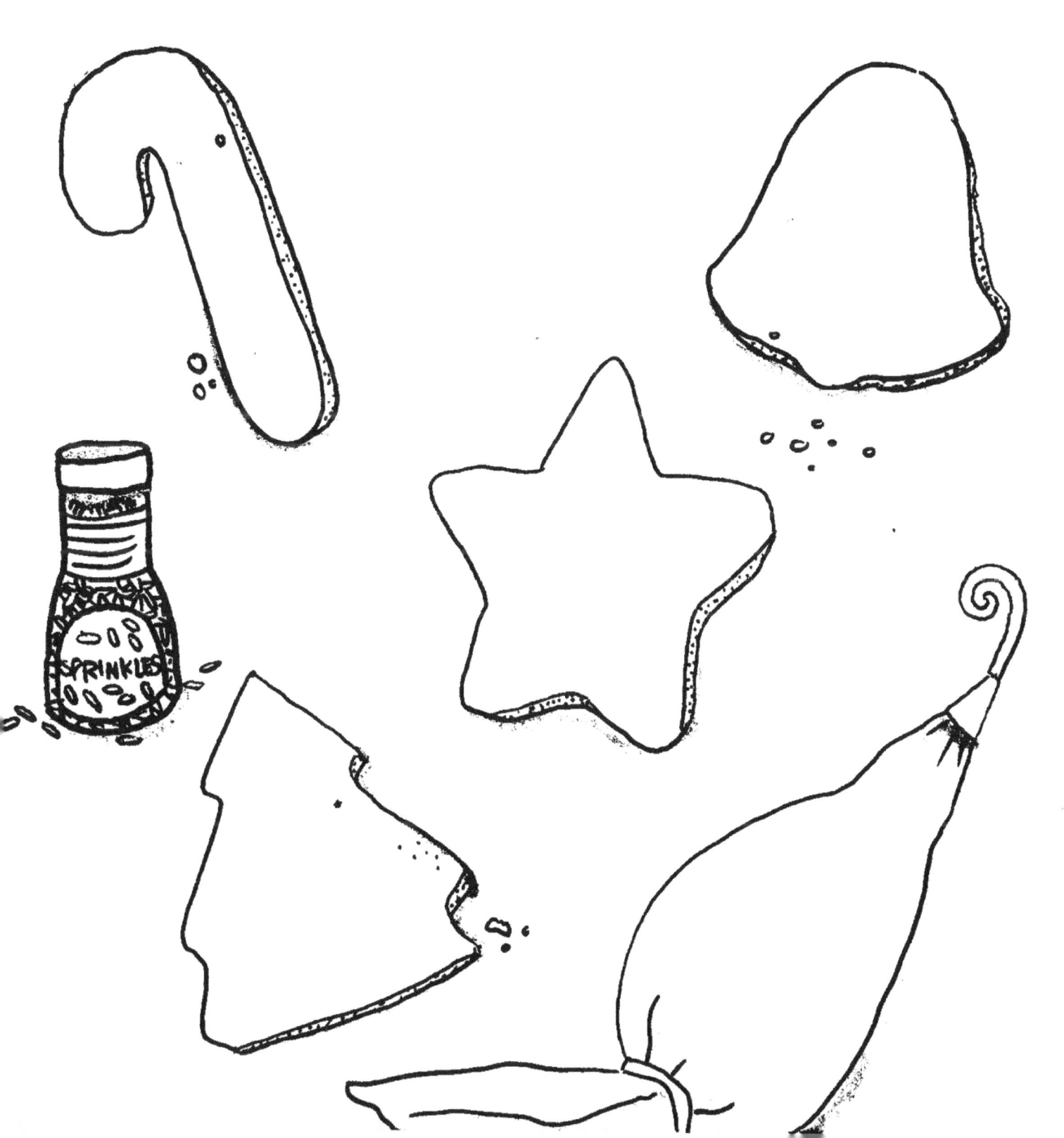

DECORATE A BIRTHDAY CAKE!

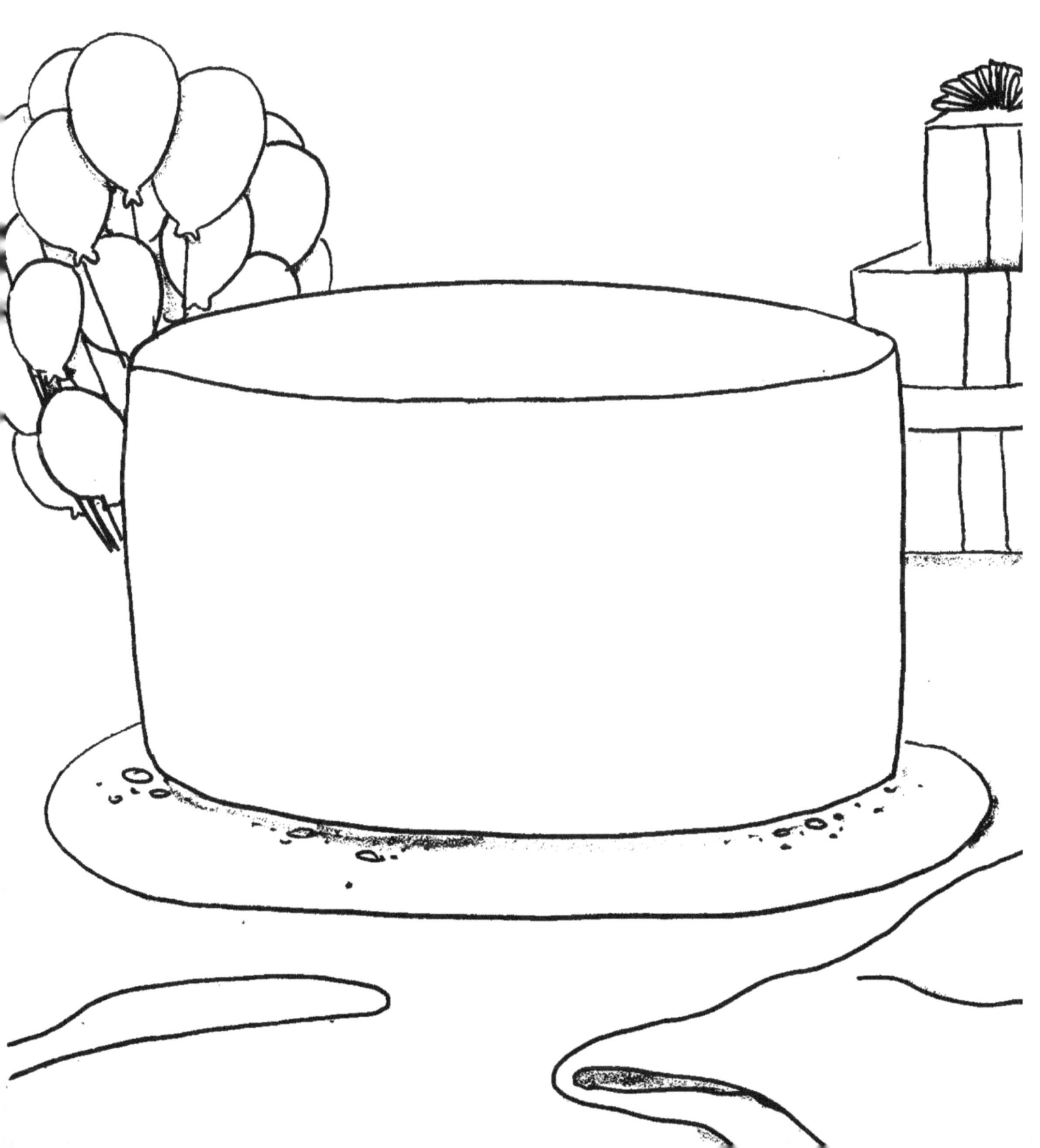

WHAT'S HATCHING OUT OF THESE EGGS?

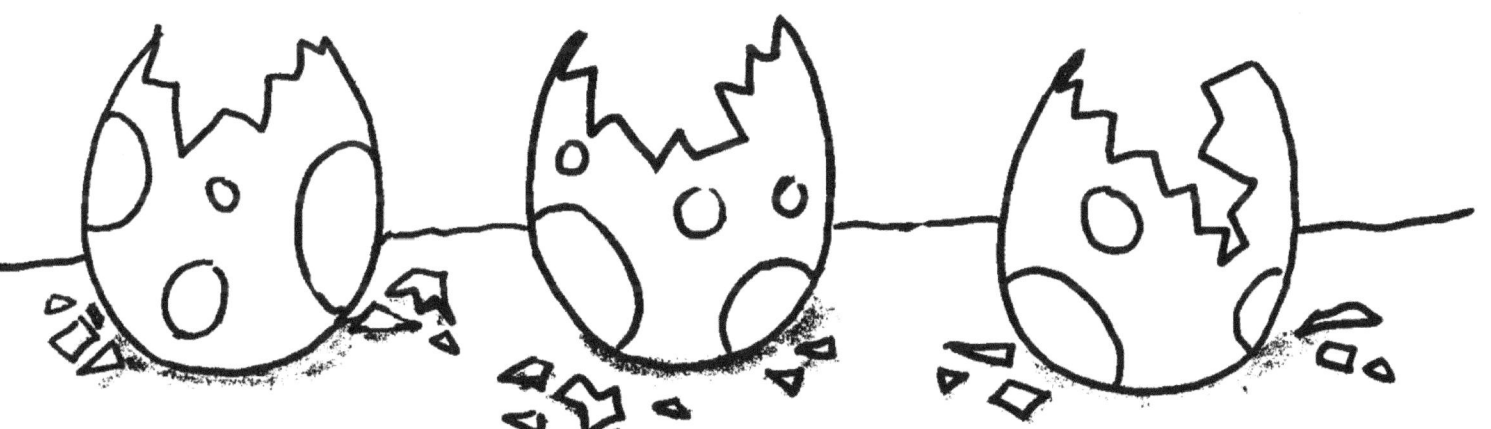

WHAT'S GROWING ON THIS TREE?

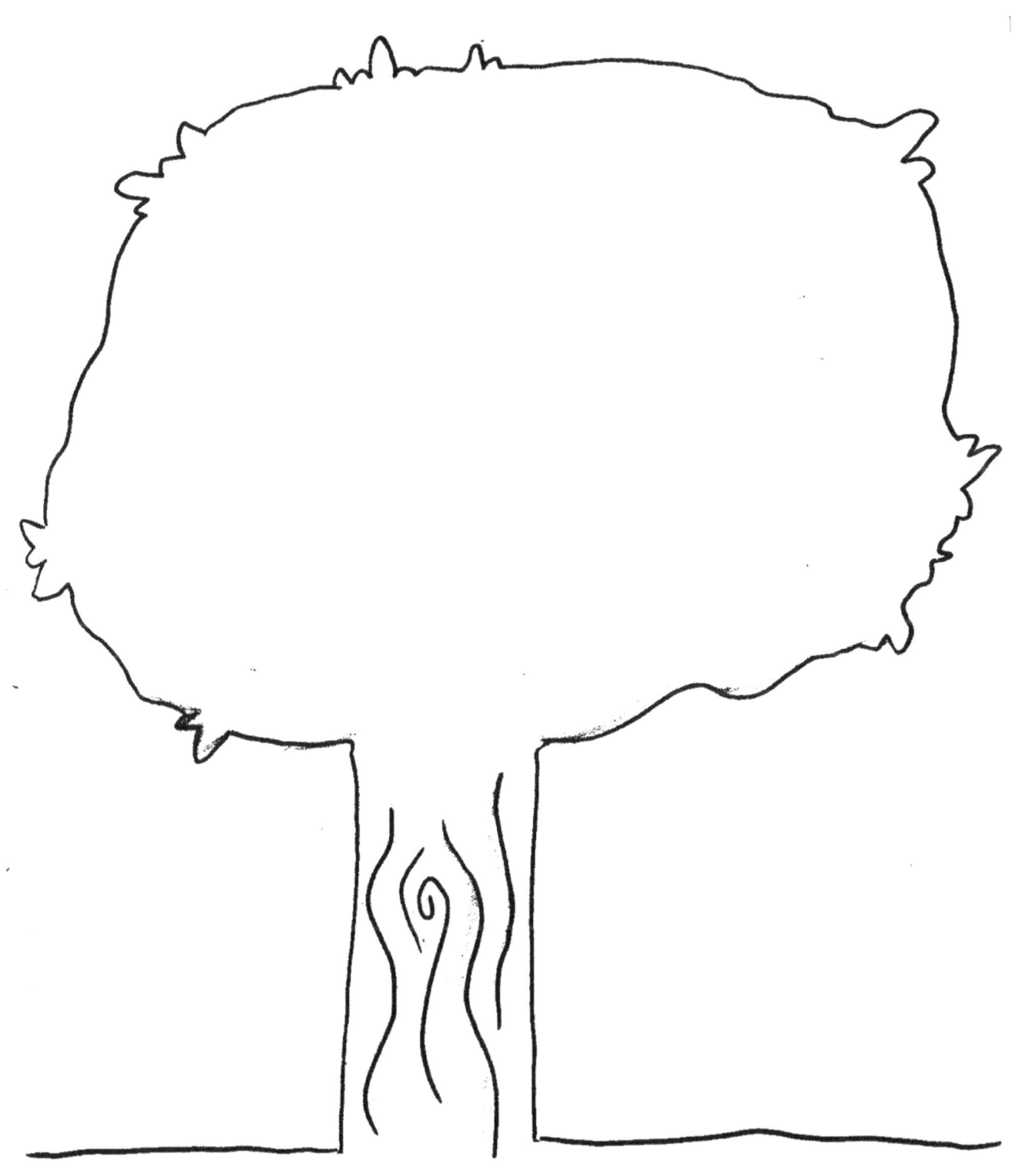

WHAT'S INSIDE THE TREASURE CHEST?

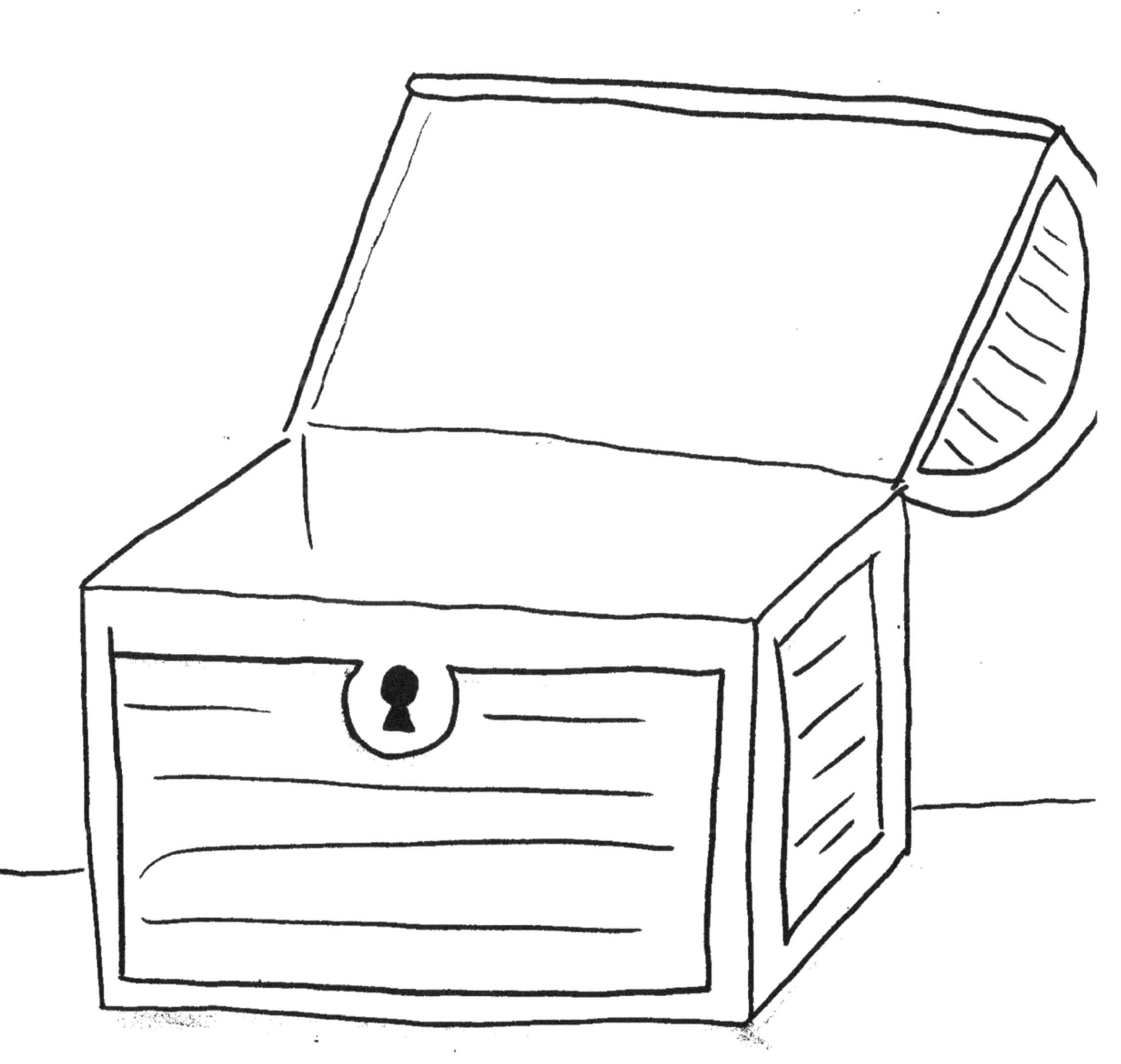

MAKE THE WORLD'S YUMMIEST PIZZA!

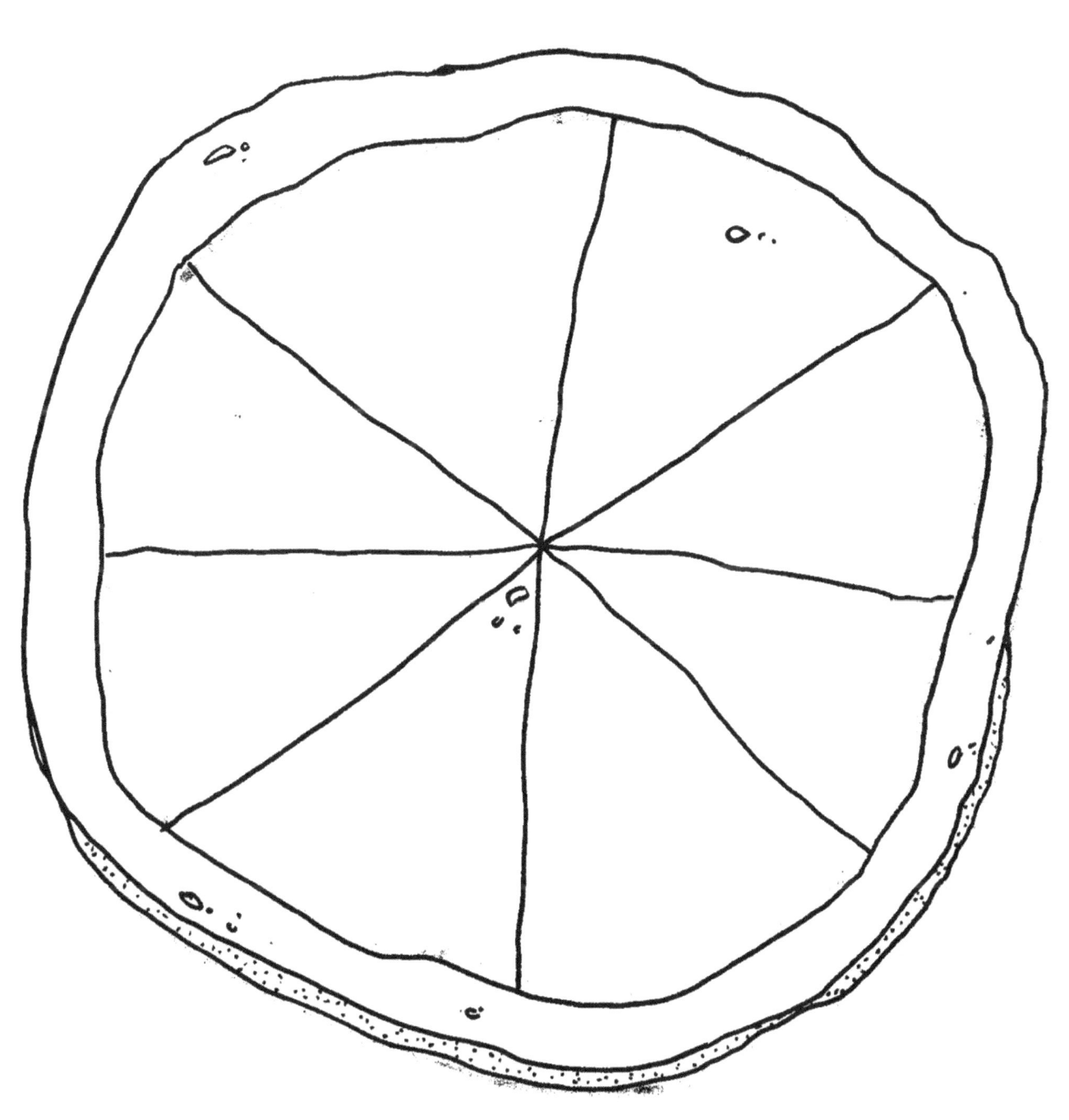

FINISH THE SILLY ALIENS!

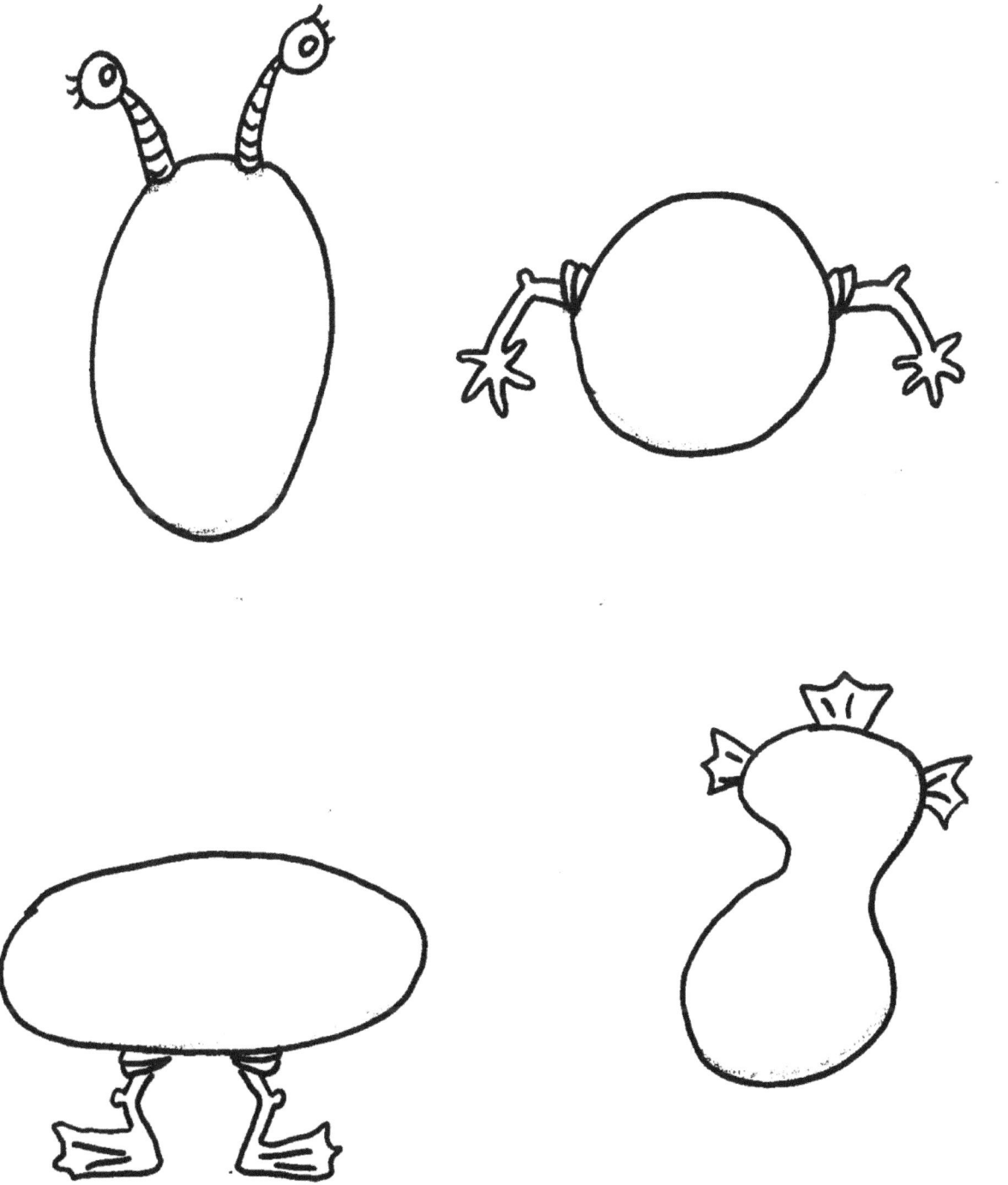

FINISH THE HORSE.

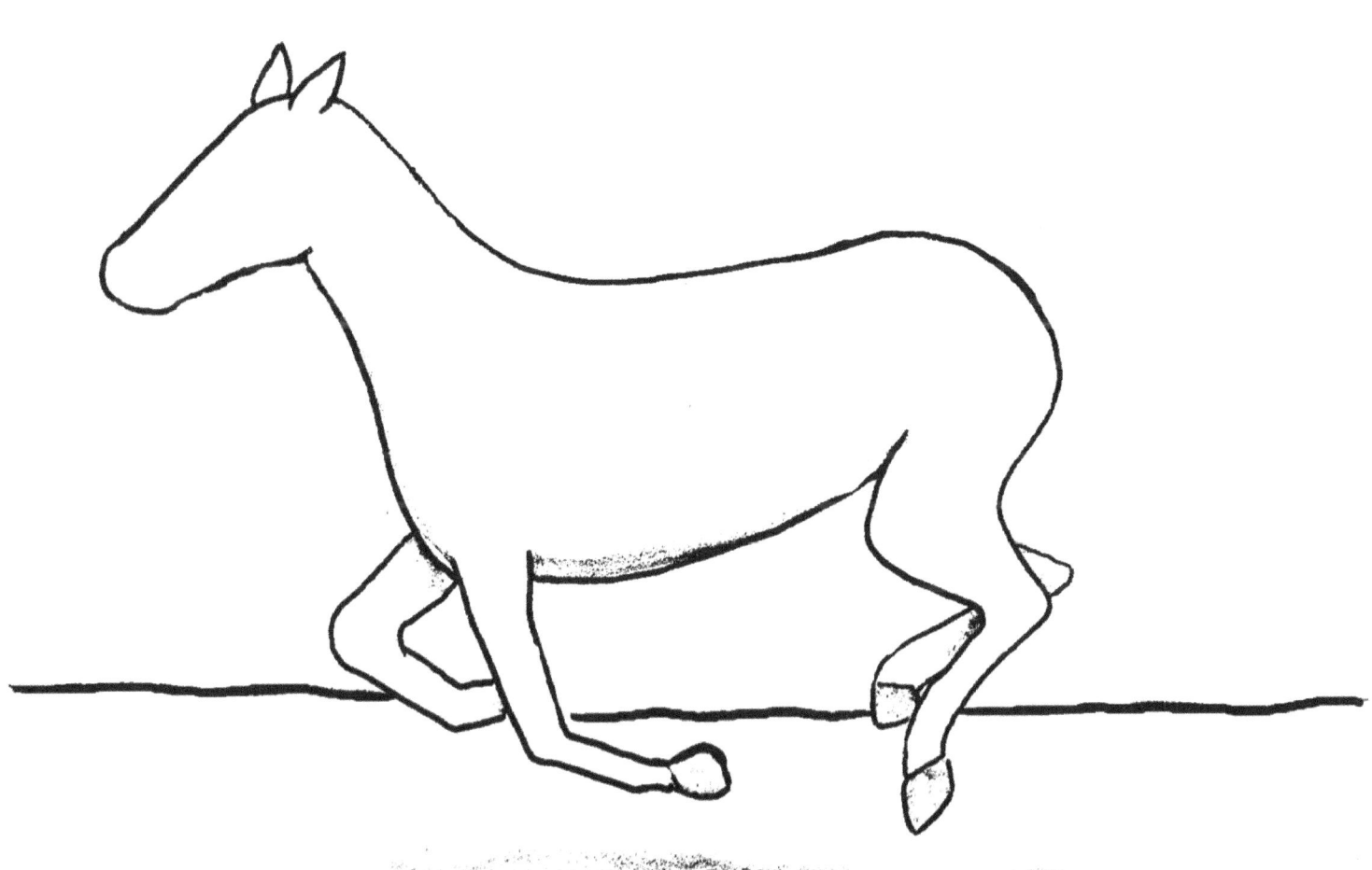

WHAT'S SWIMMING IN HERE?

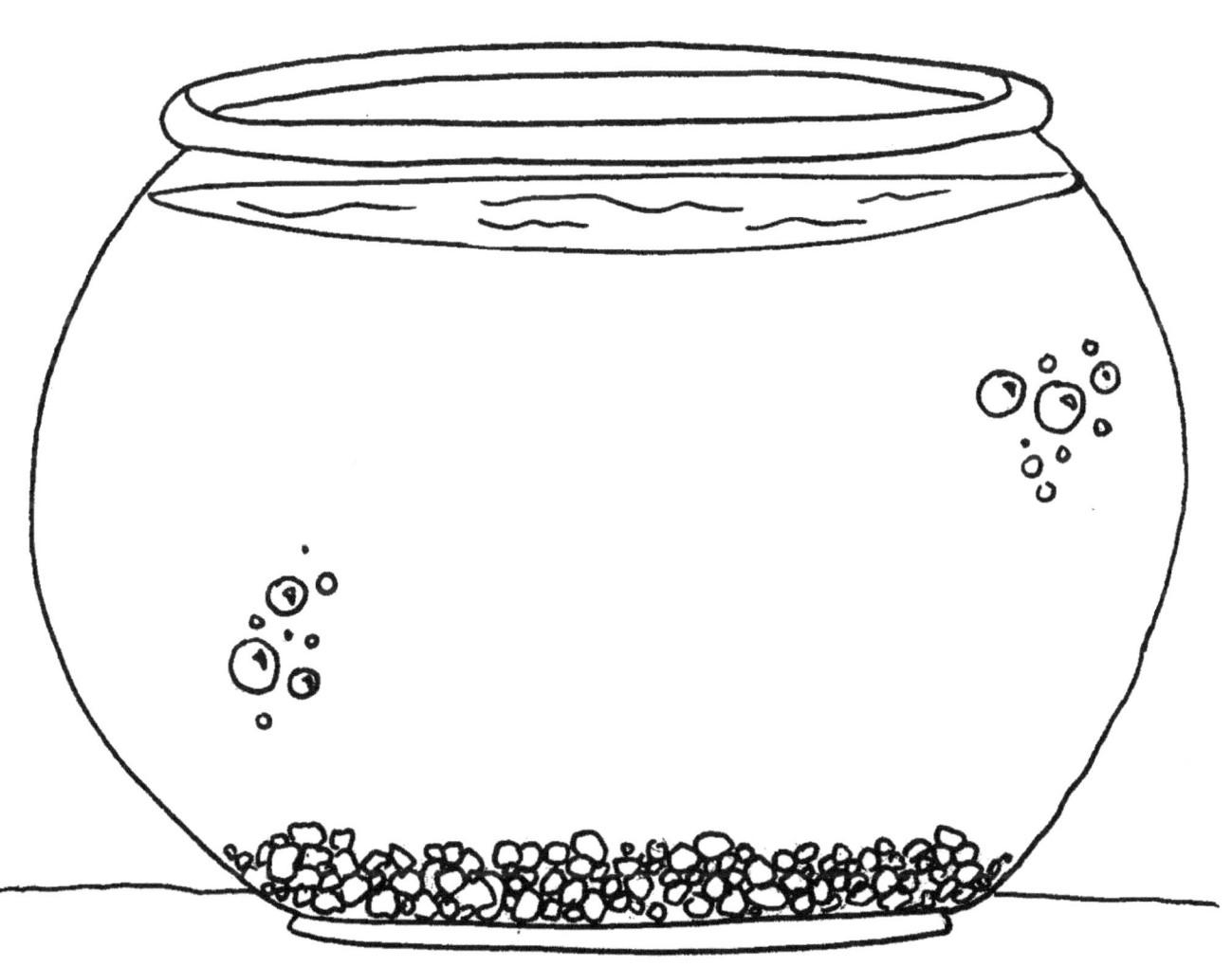

WHO'S IN THE MIRROR?

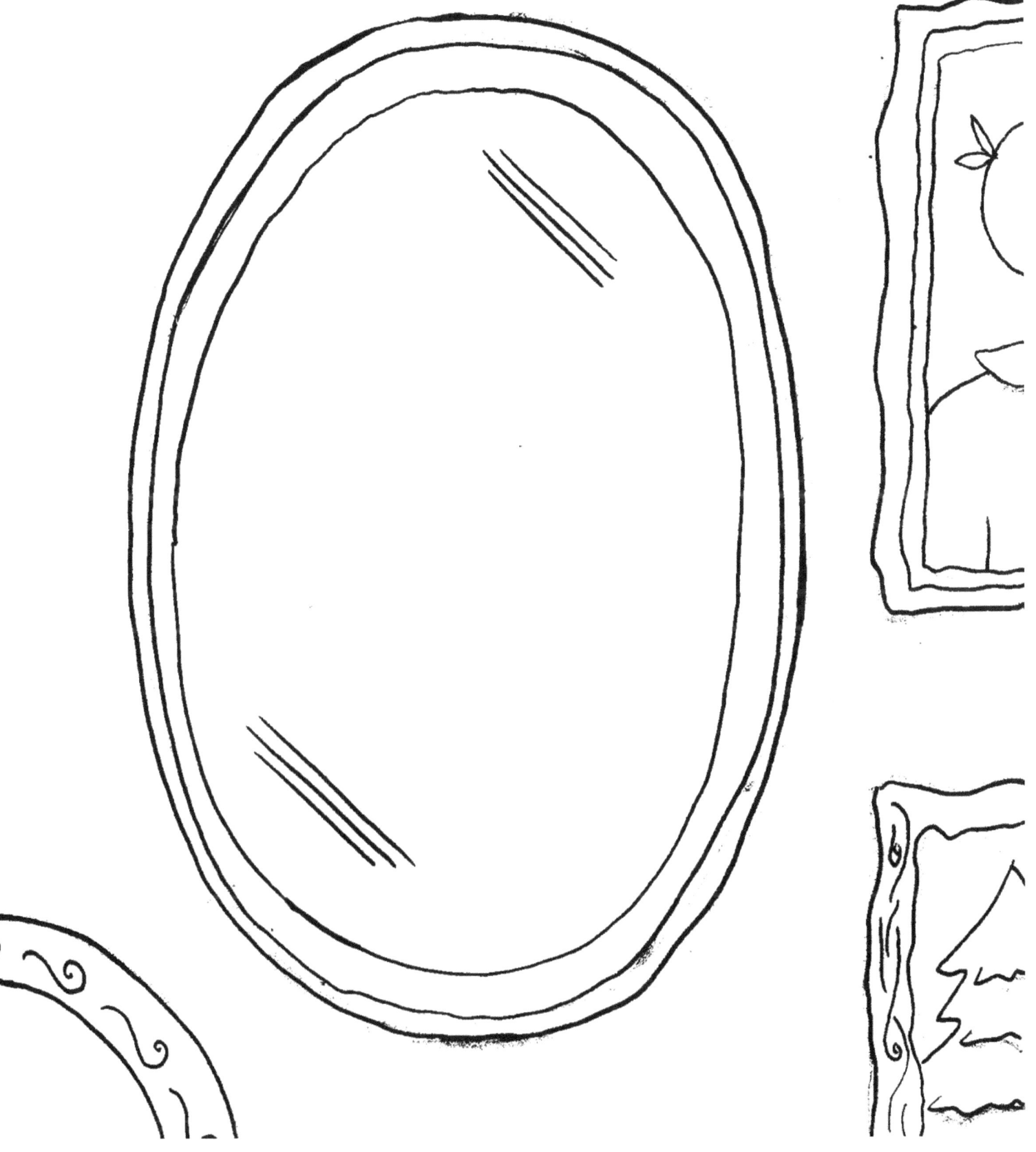

WHO'S SURFING?

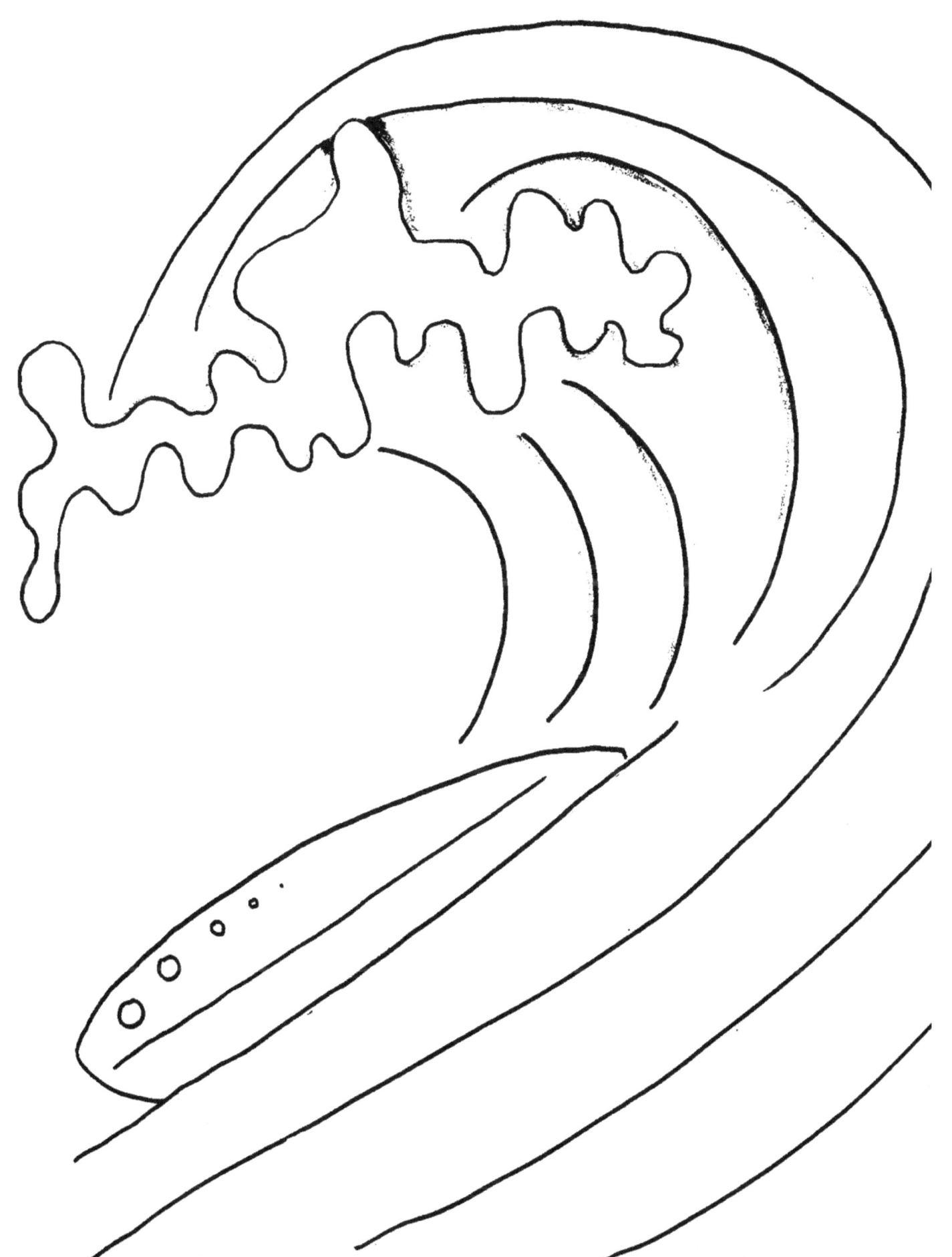

ADD SOME DELICIOUS TOPPINGS!

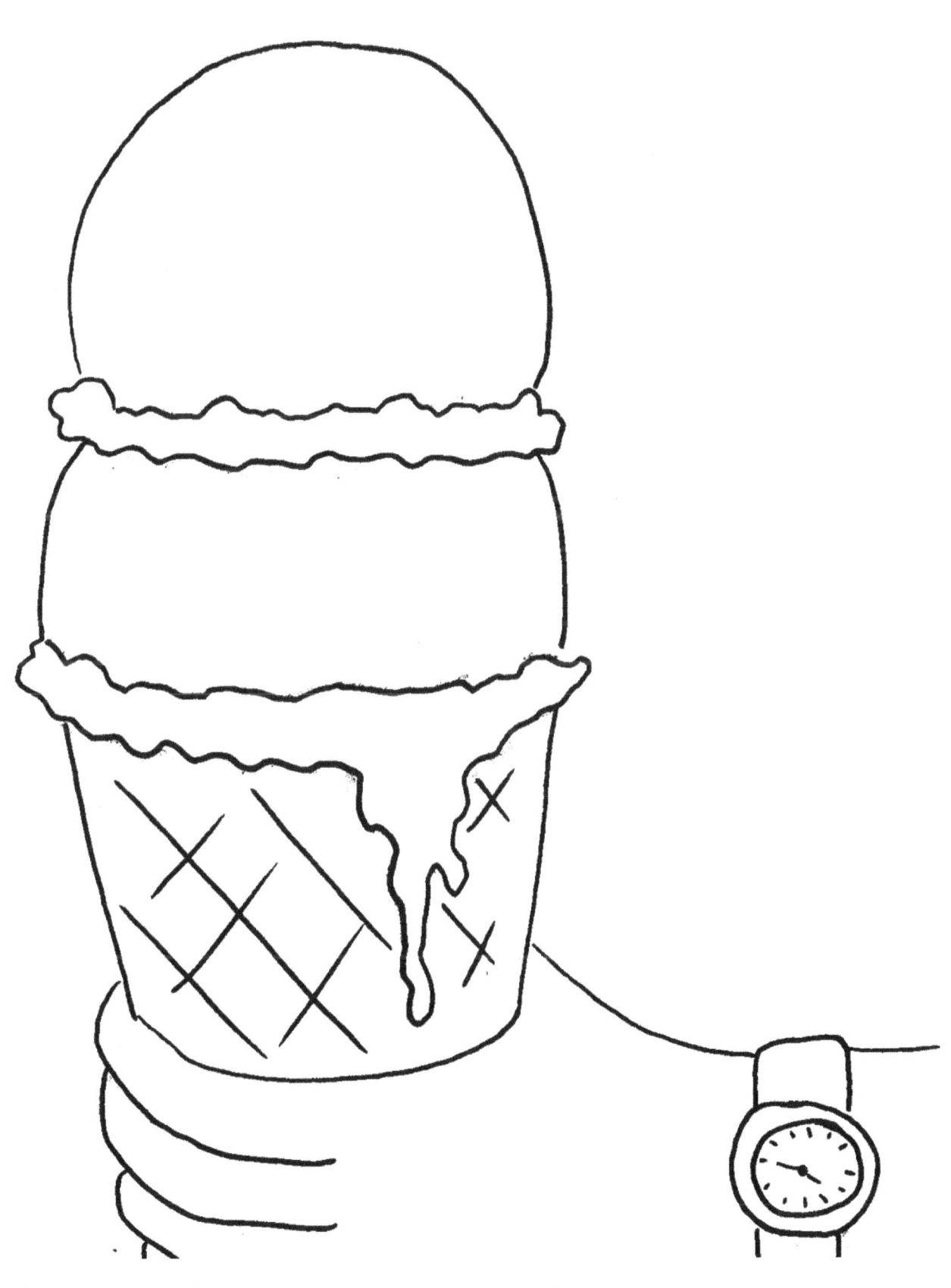

CAN YOU DRAW THE OPPOSITE?

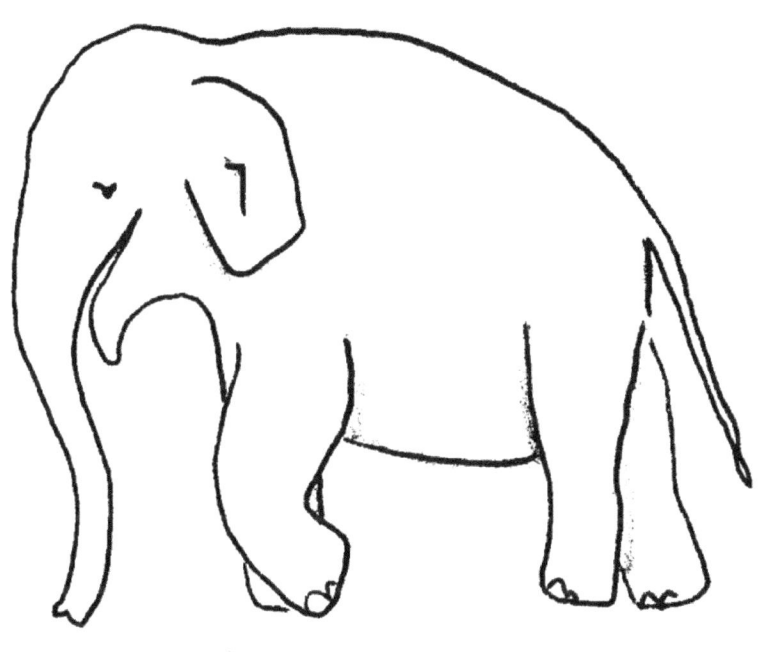

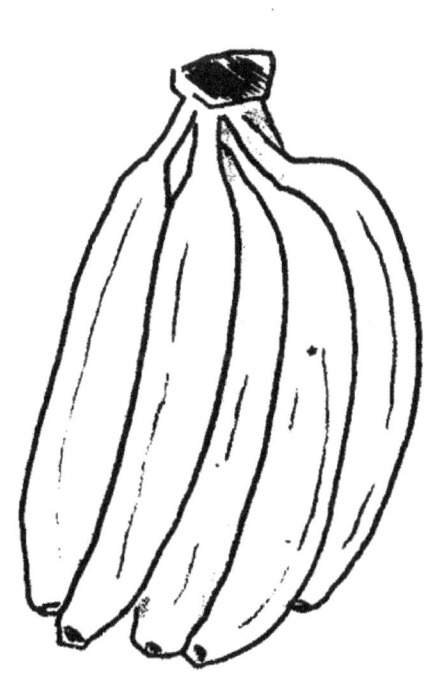

WHAT IS THIS STOMACH DIGESTING?

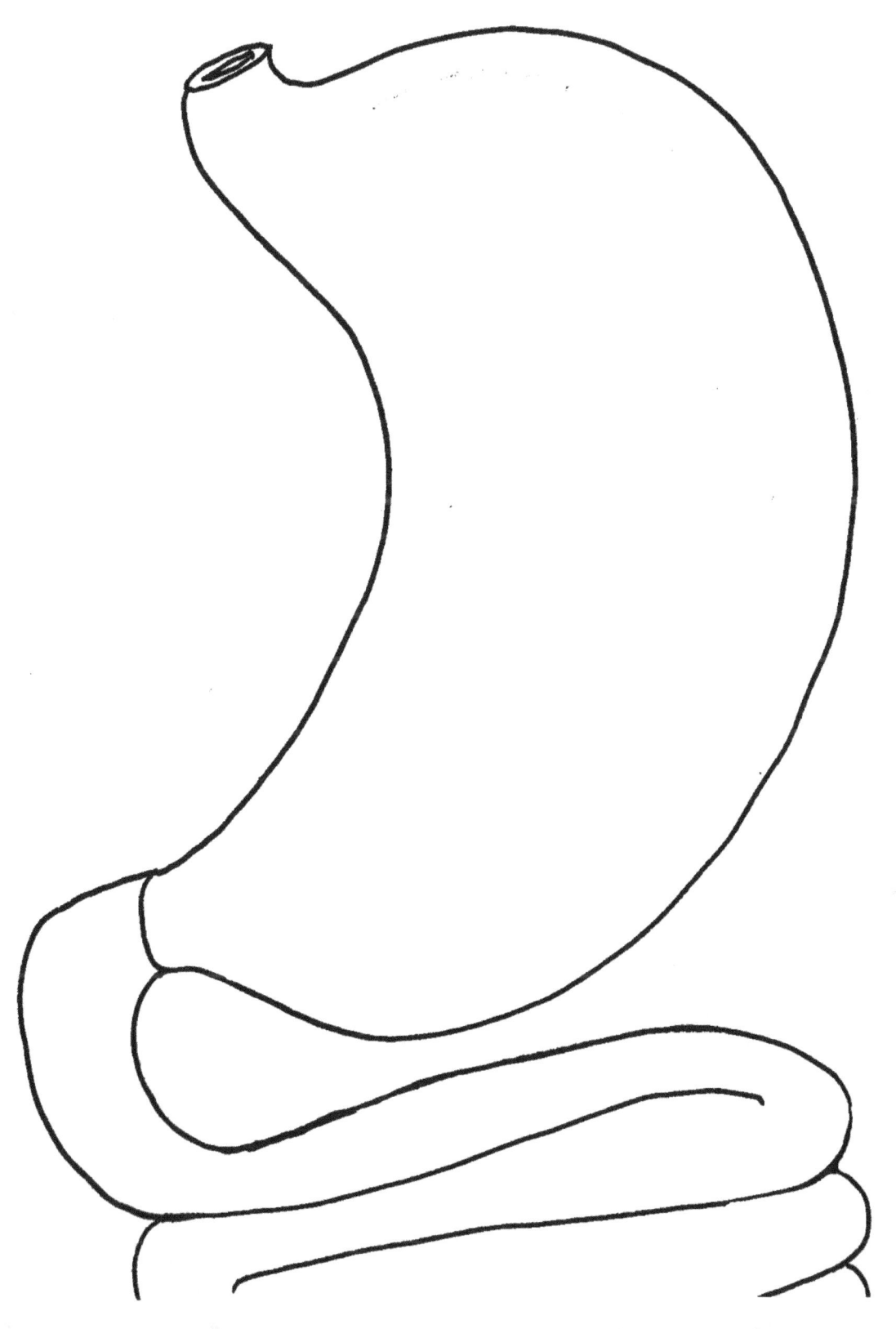

DRAW YOUR OWN PLANET!

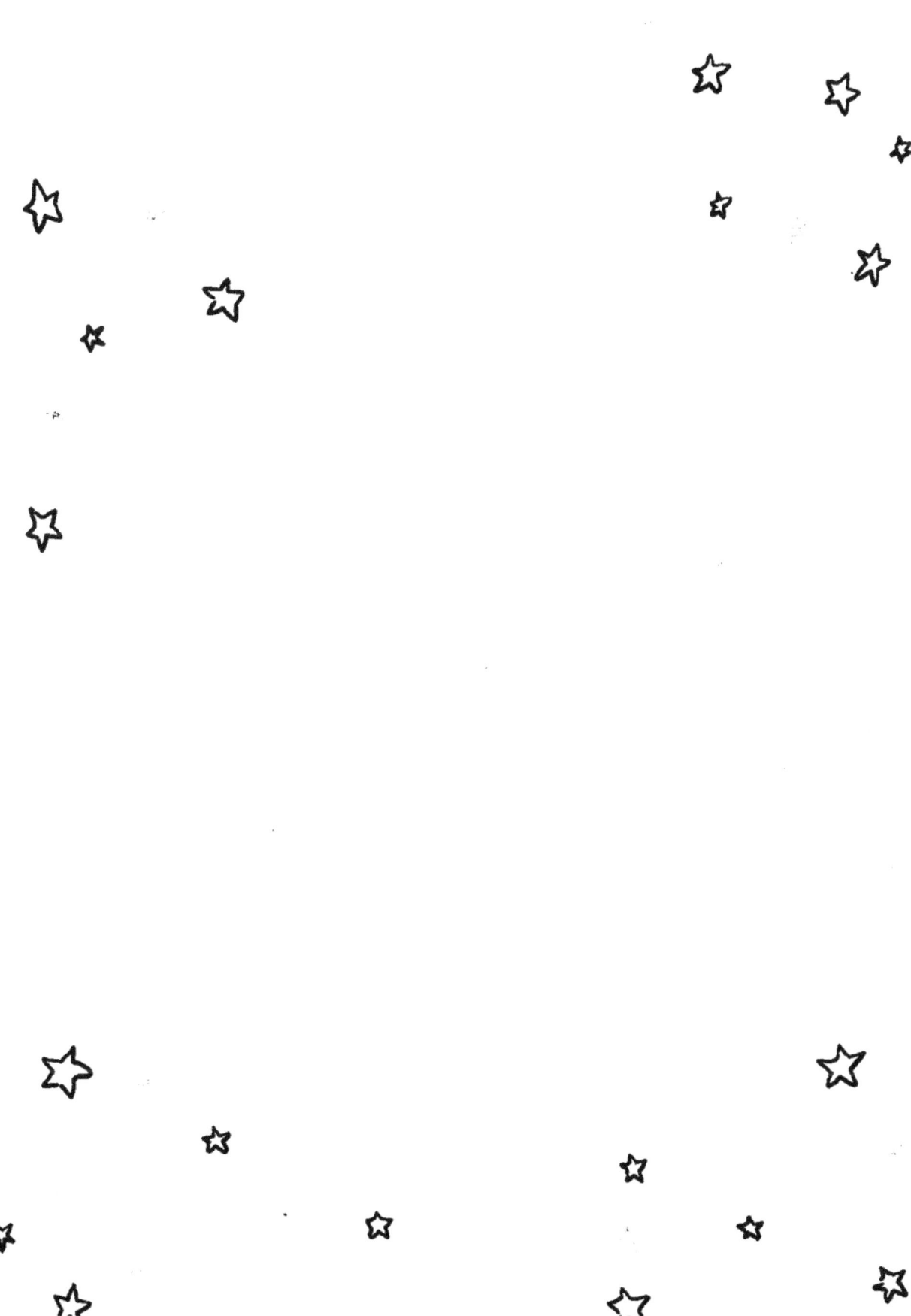

WHO'S HIDING IN THIS UNDERWATER CAVE?

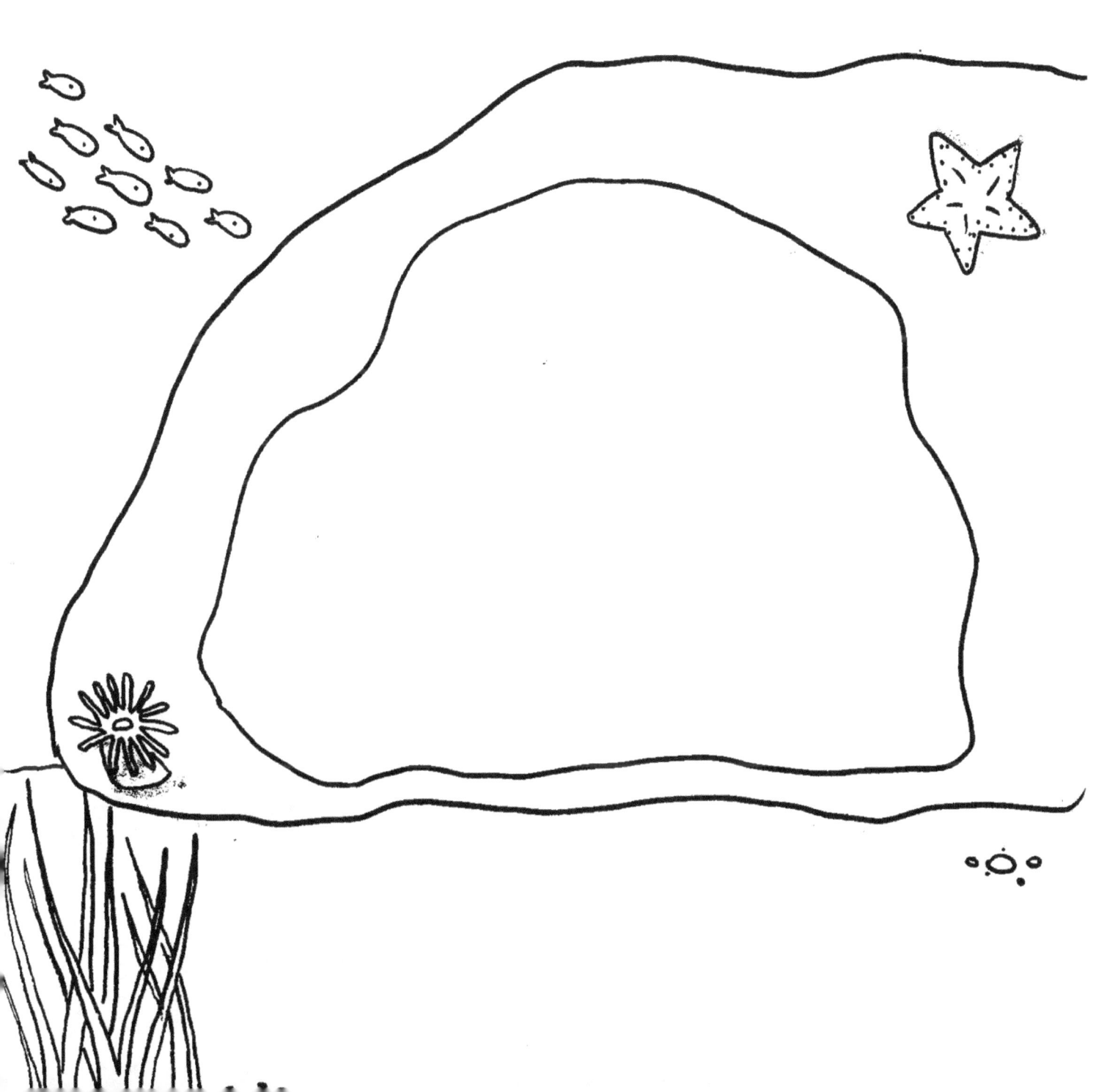

GIVE HER WINGS!

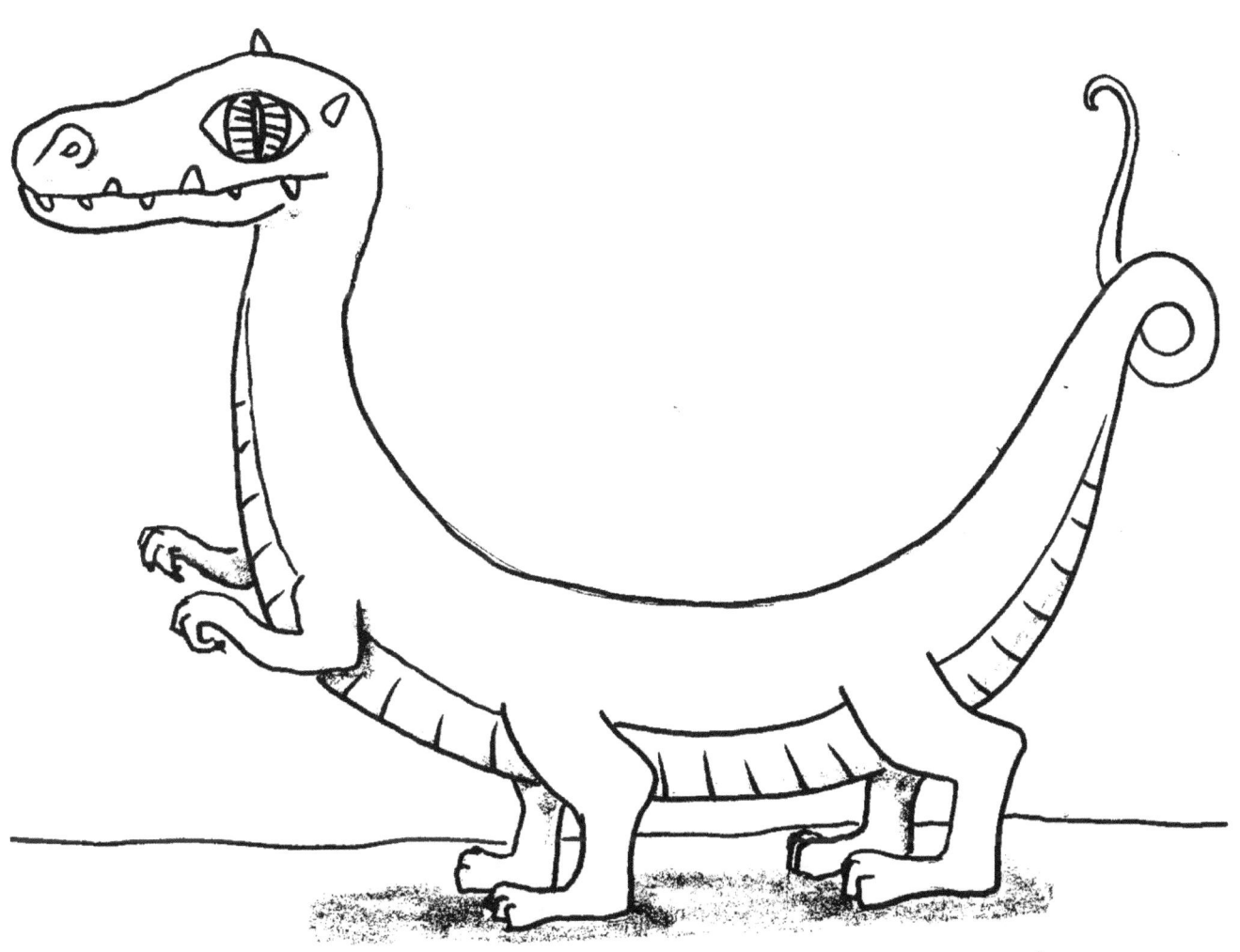

GIVE THIS PUMPKIN A SPOOKY FACE.

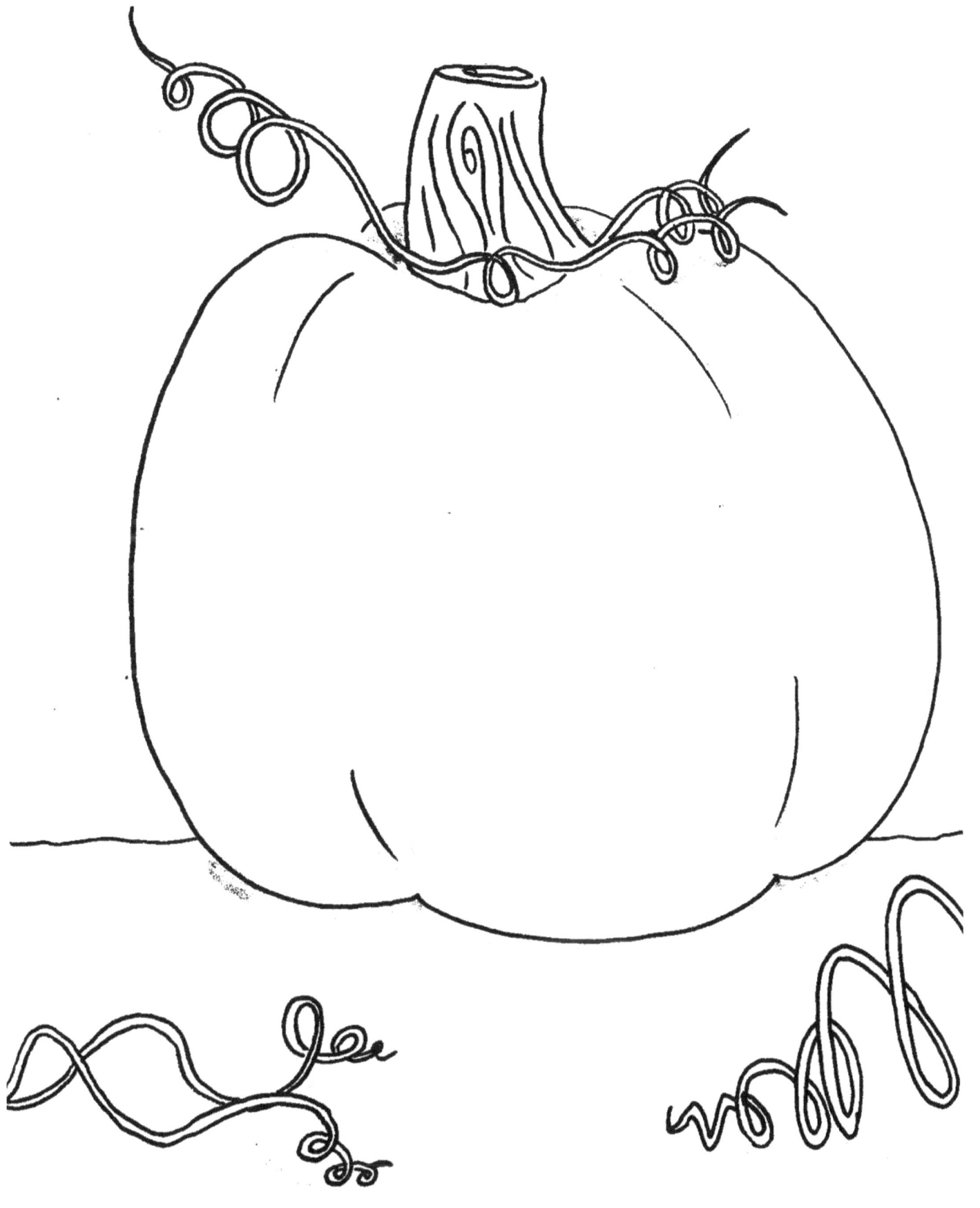

WHAT'S HIDING FROM THE DOG?

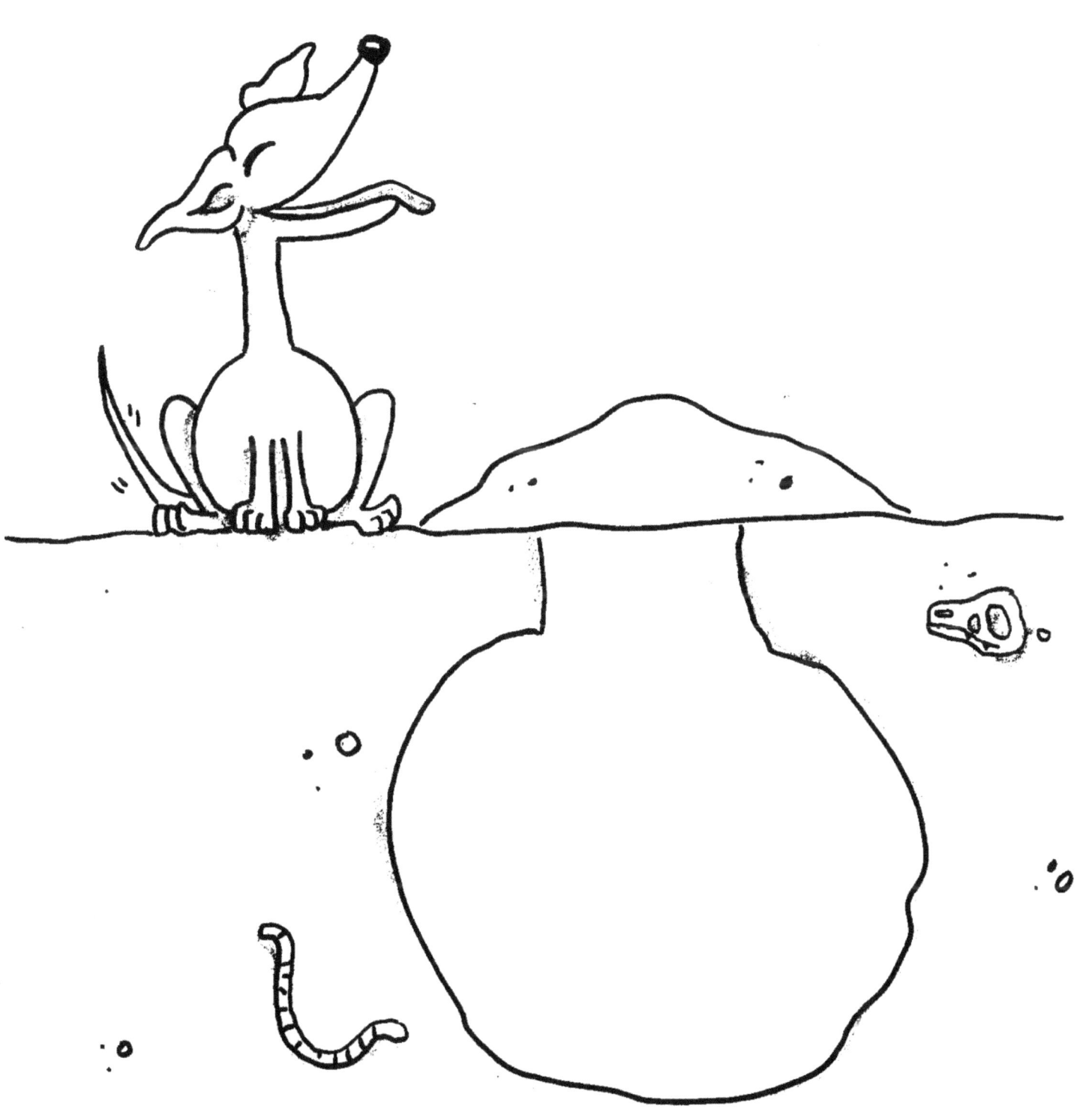

ADD SOME FURNITURE TO THE BIRD'S LIVING ROOM.

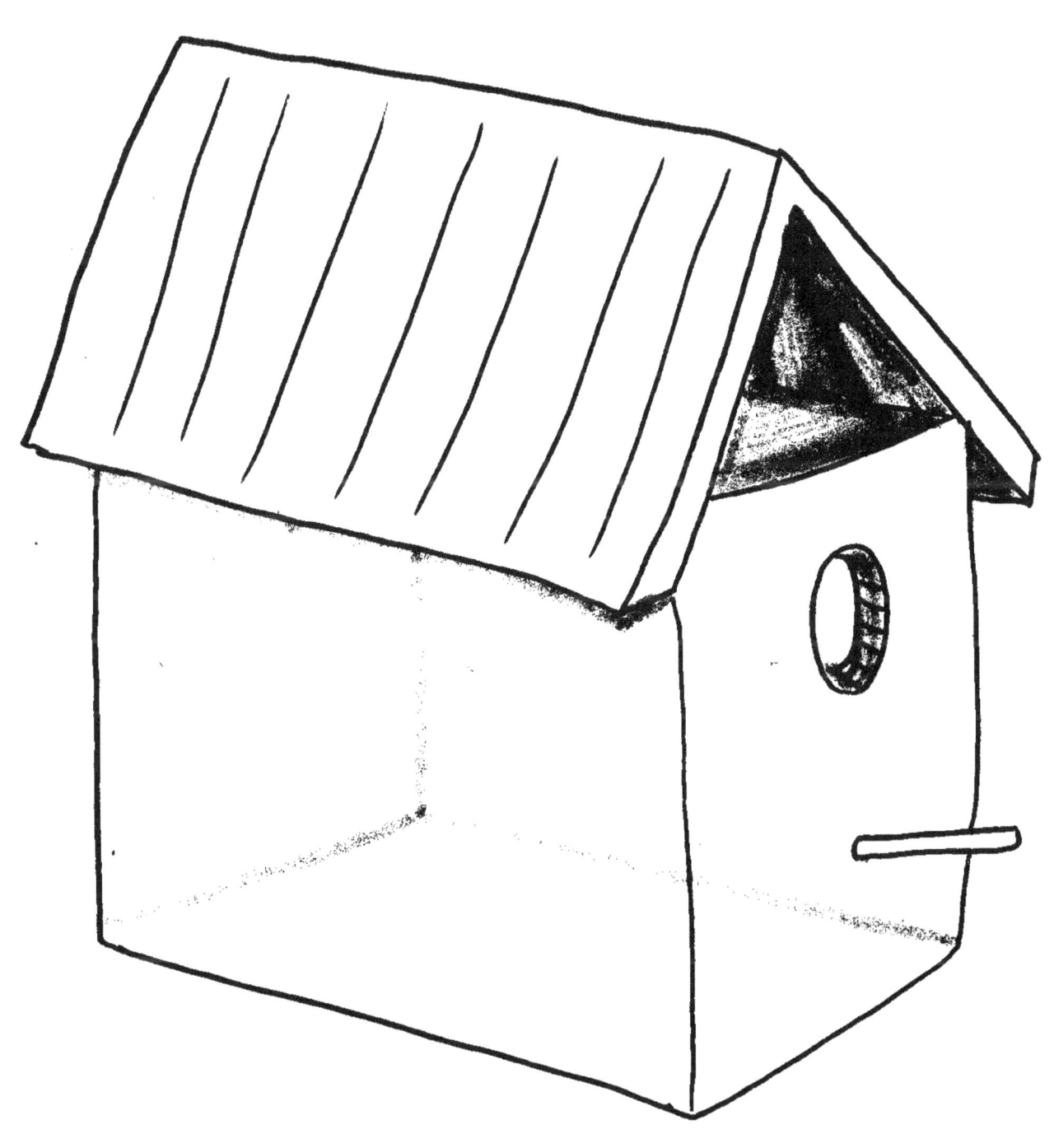

WHAT'S FOR BREAKFAST?

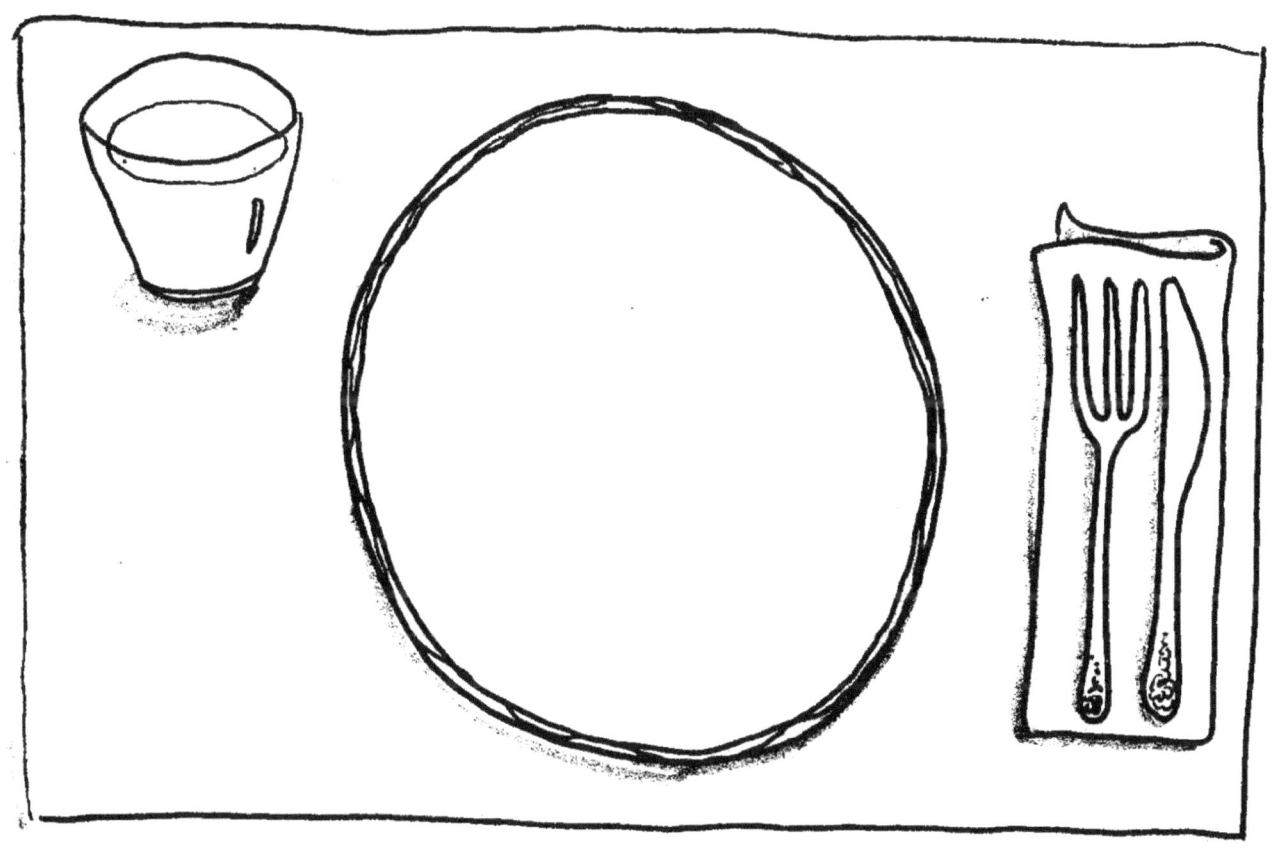

ADD A SLEEPY SQUIRREL.

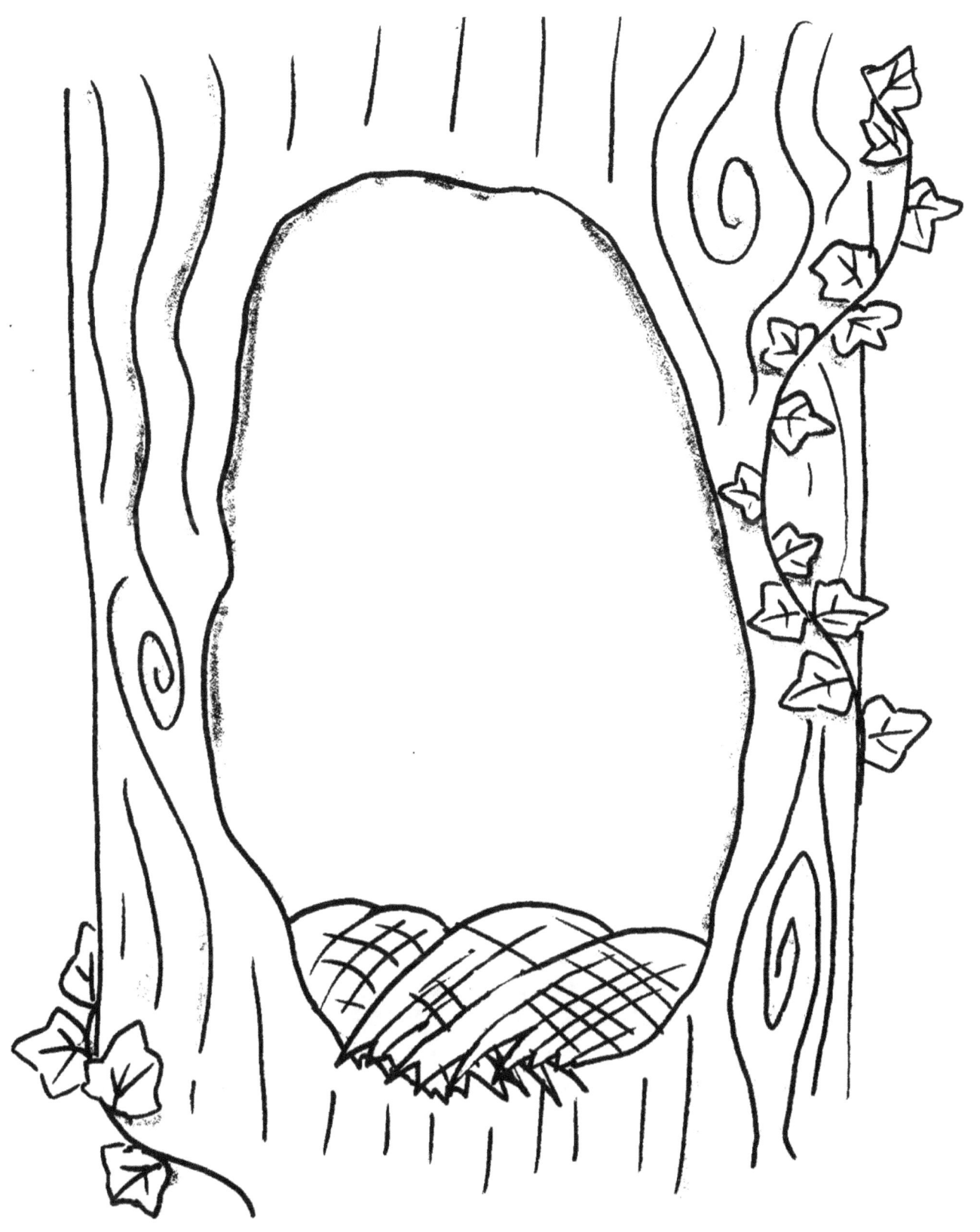

WHAT DOES THE DOG KEEP INSIDE HIS HOUSE?

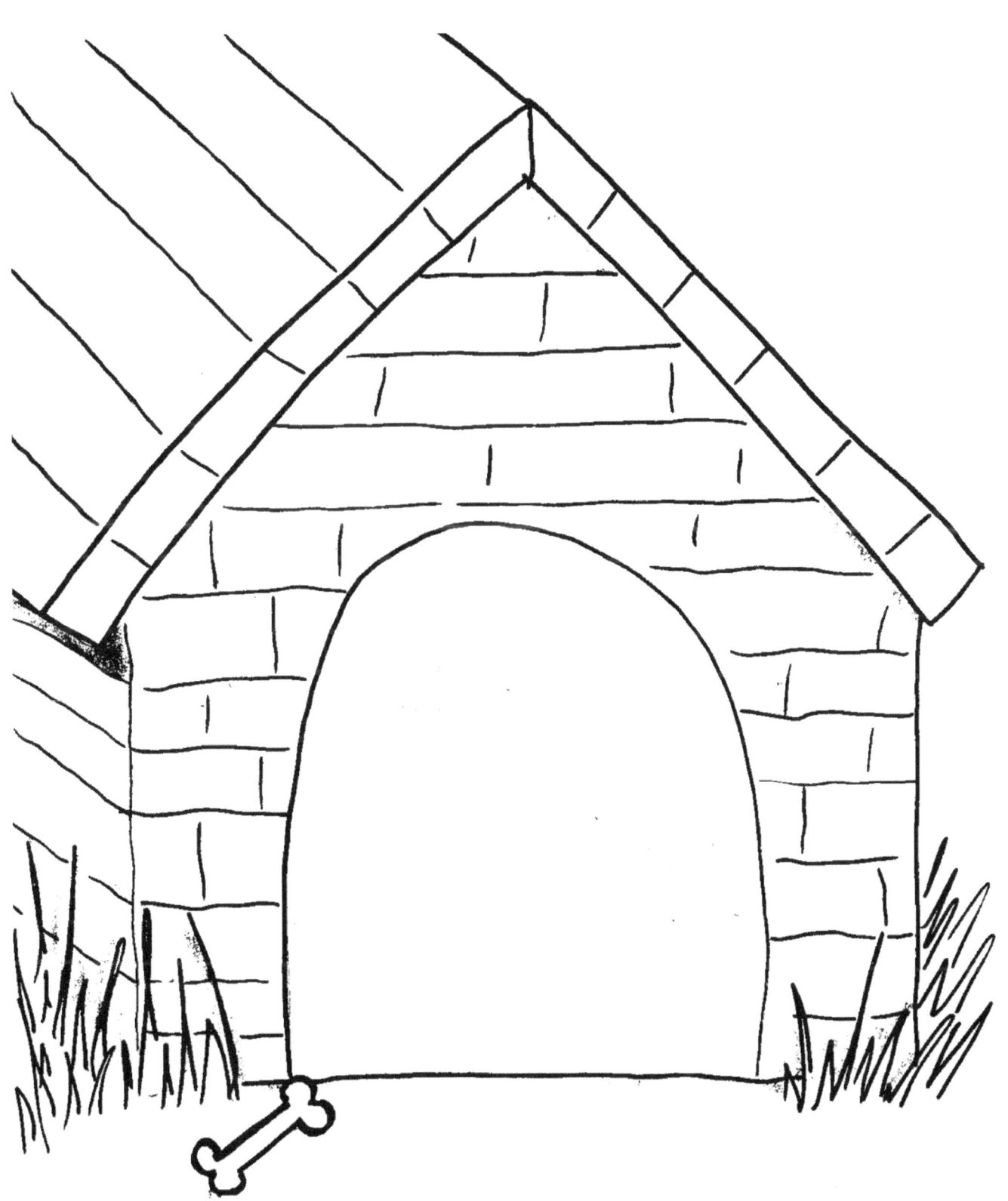

MAKE IT A VENUS FLYTRAP.

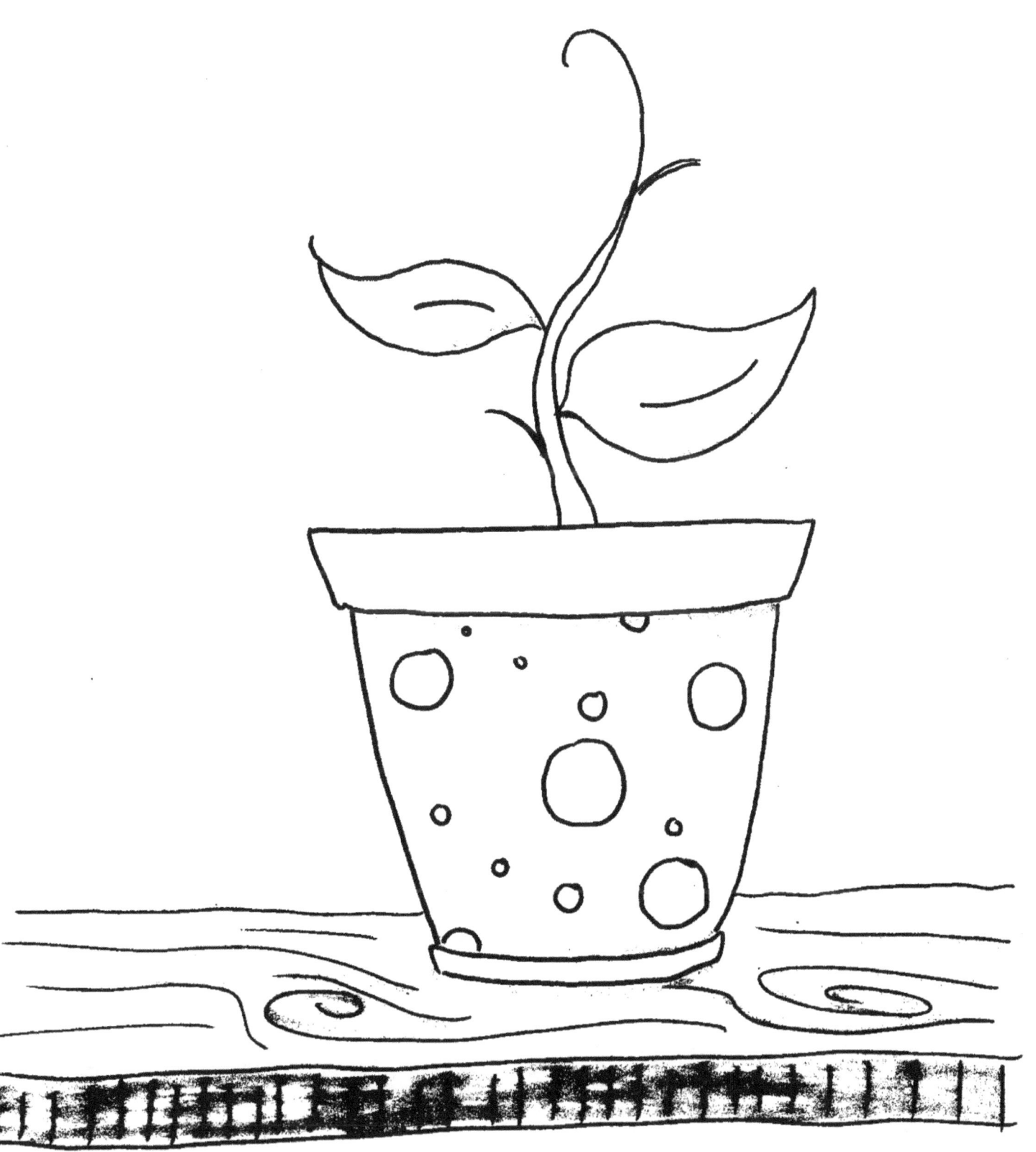

THE SPIDER HAS CAUGHT 5 BUGS- WHAT ARE THEY?

DECORATE SOME MORE COOKIES!

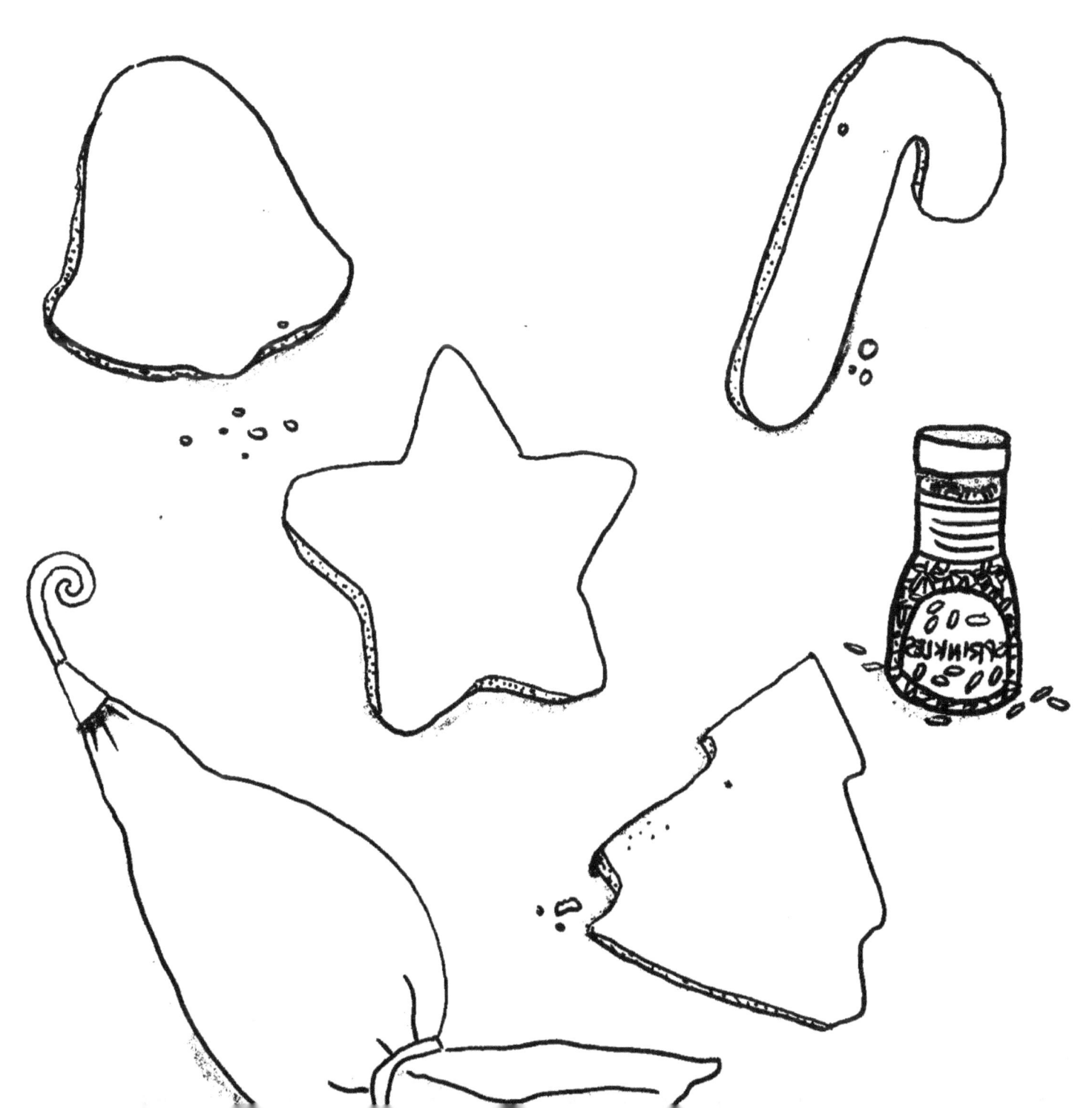

DECORATE THE WORLD'S GROSSEST CAKE.

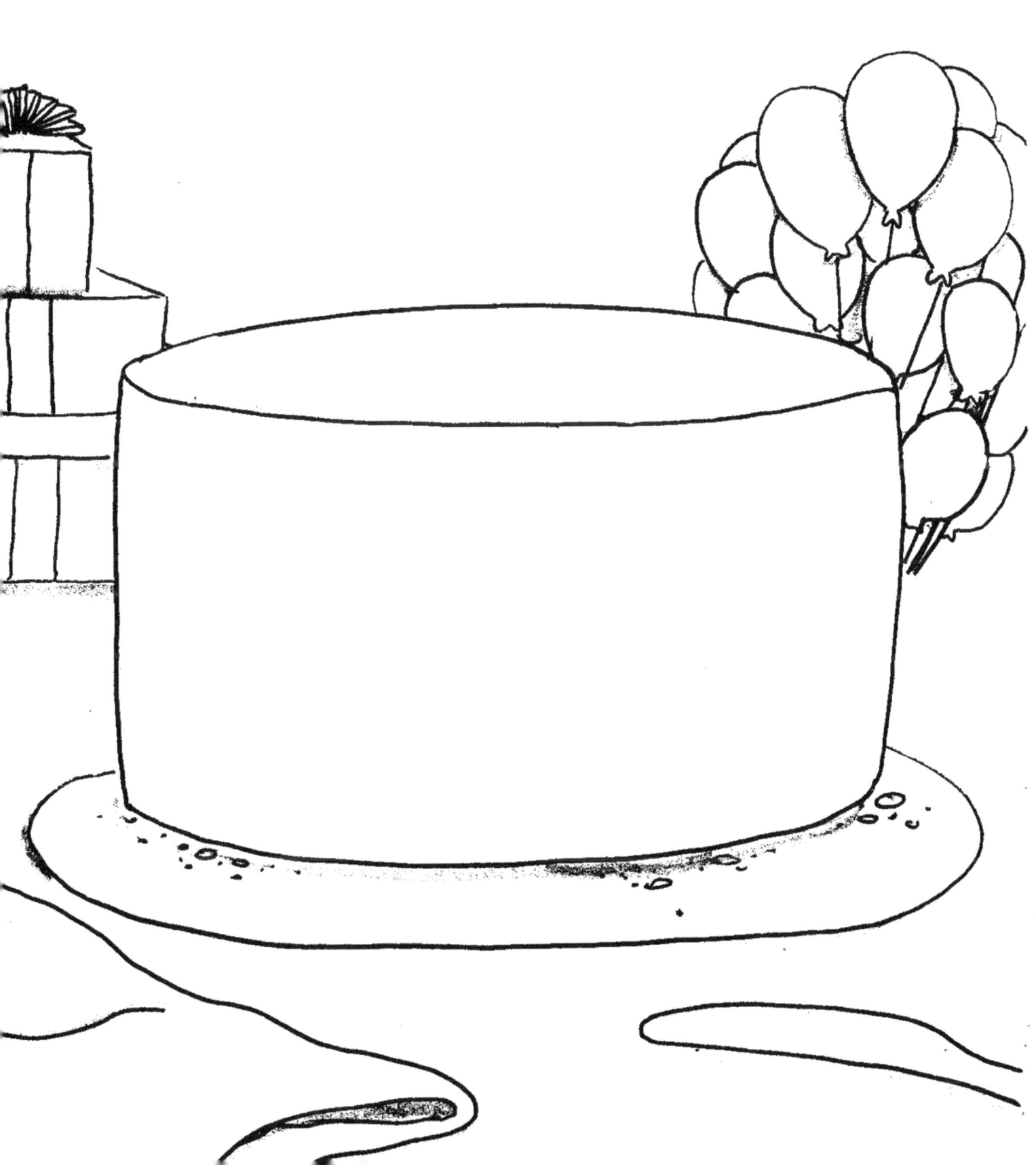

THREE BABY DRAGONS- WHAT DO THEY LOOK LIKE?

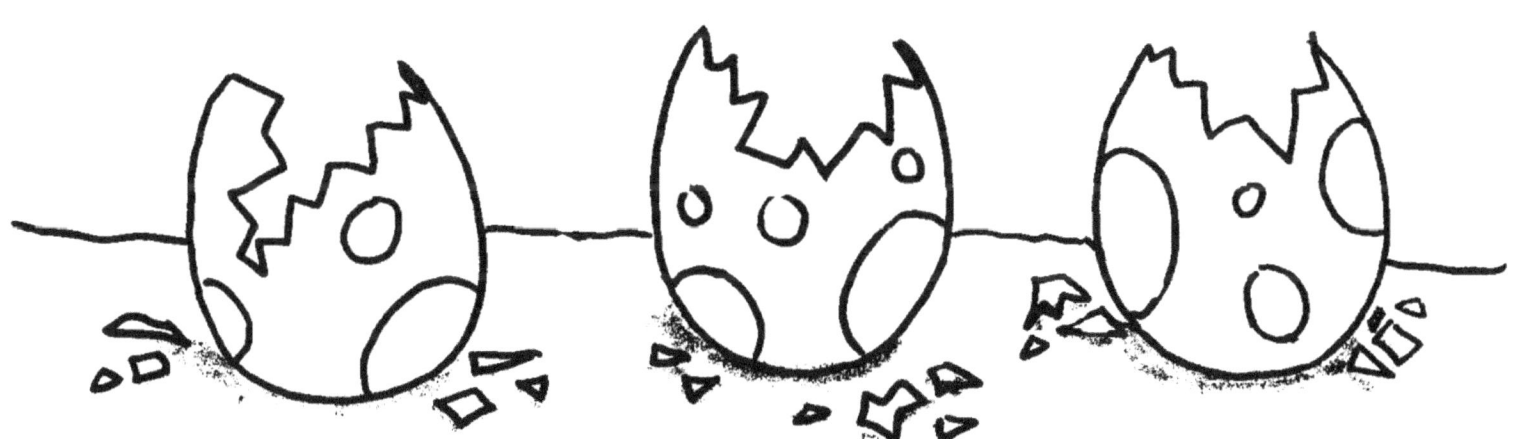

WHAT IS LIVING AMONG THE LEAVES?

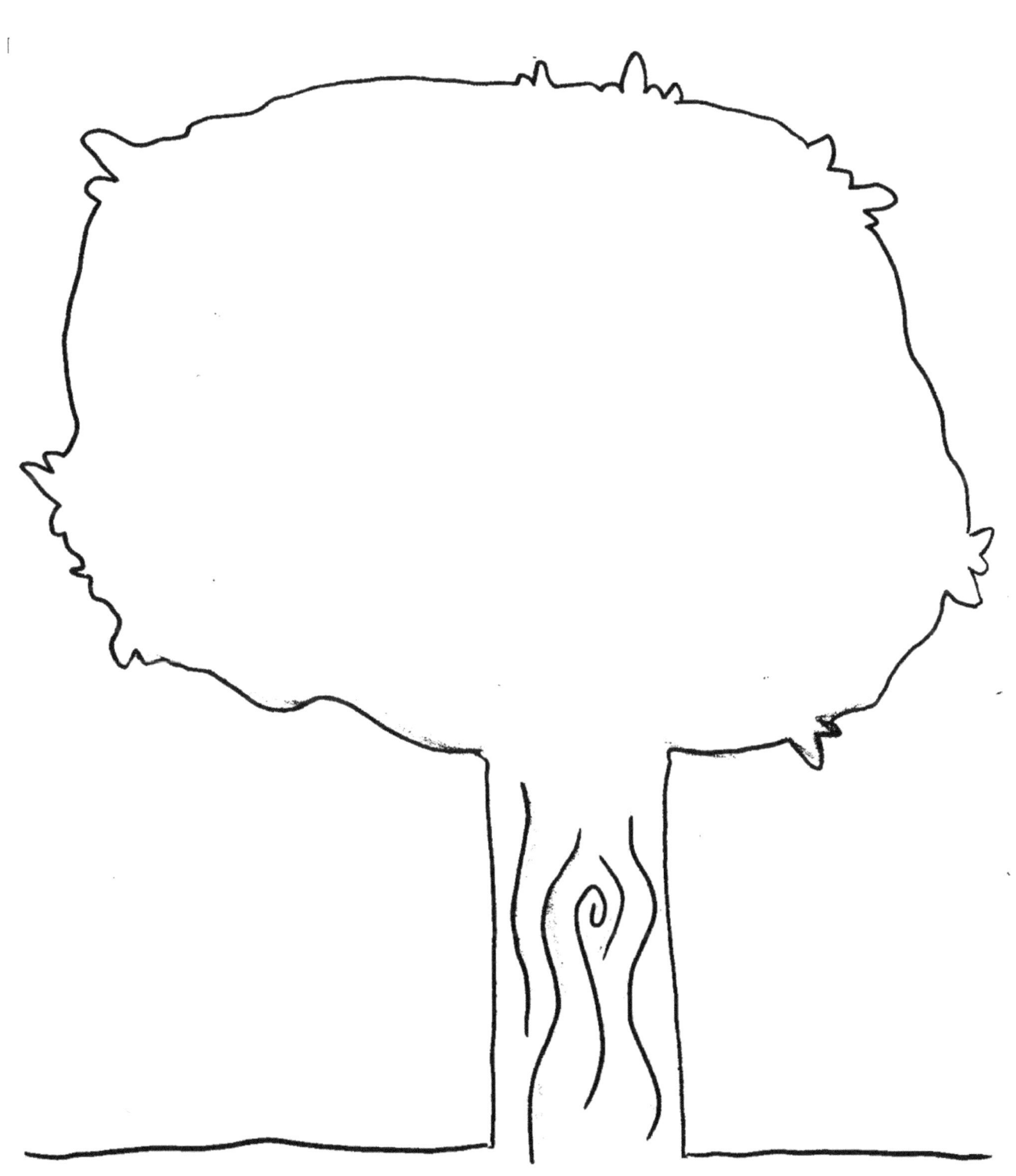

WHAT'S INSIDE THE TOY BOX?

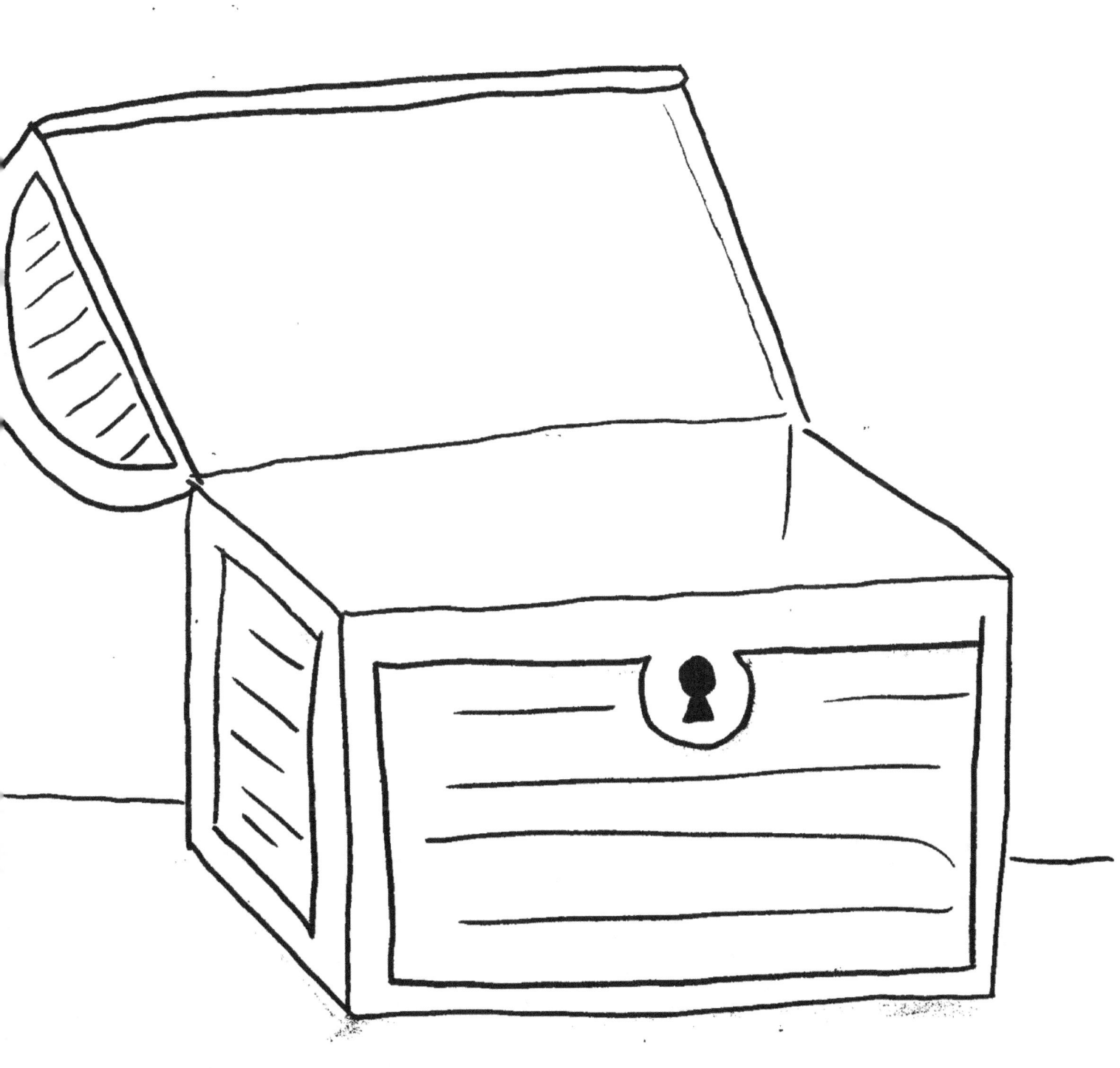

MAKE THE WORLD'S YUCKIEST PIZZA!

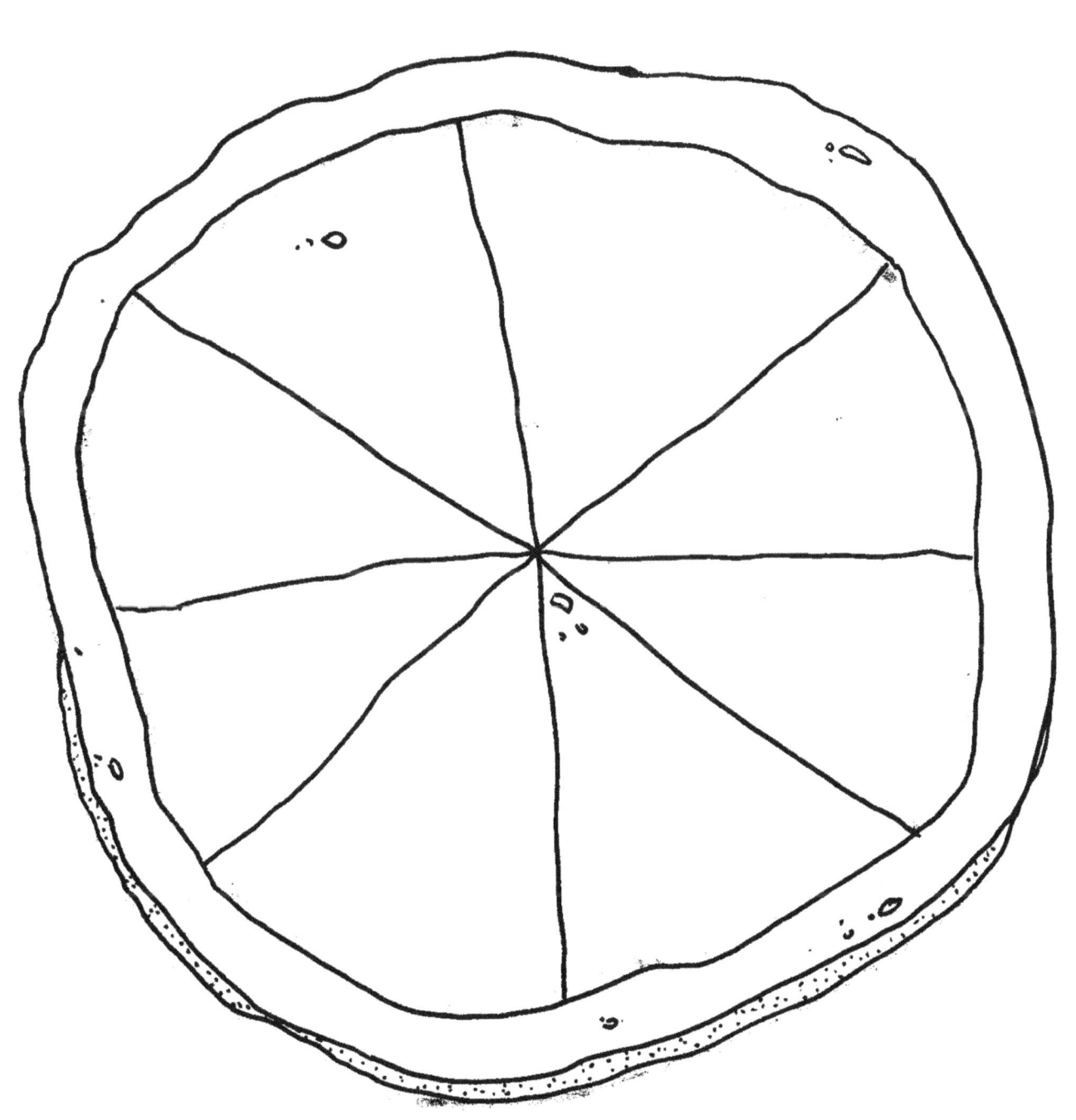

FINISH THE MEAN ALIENS!

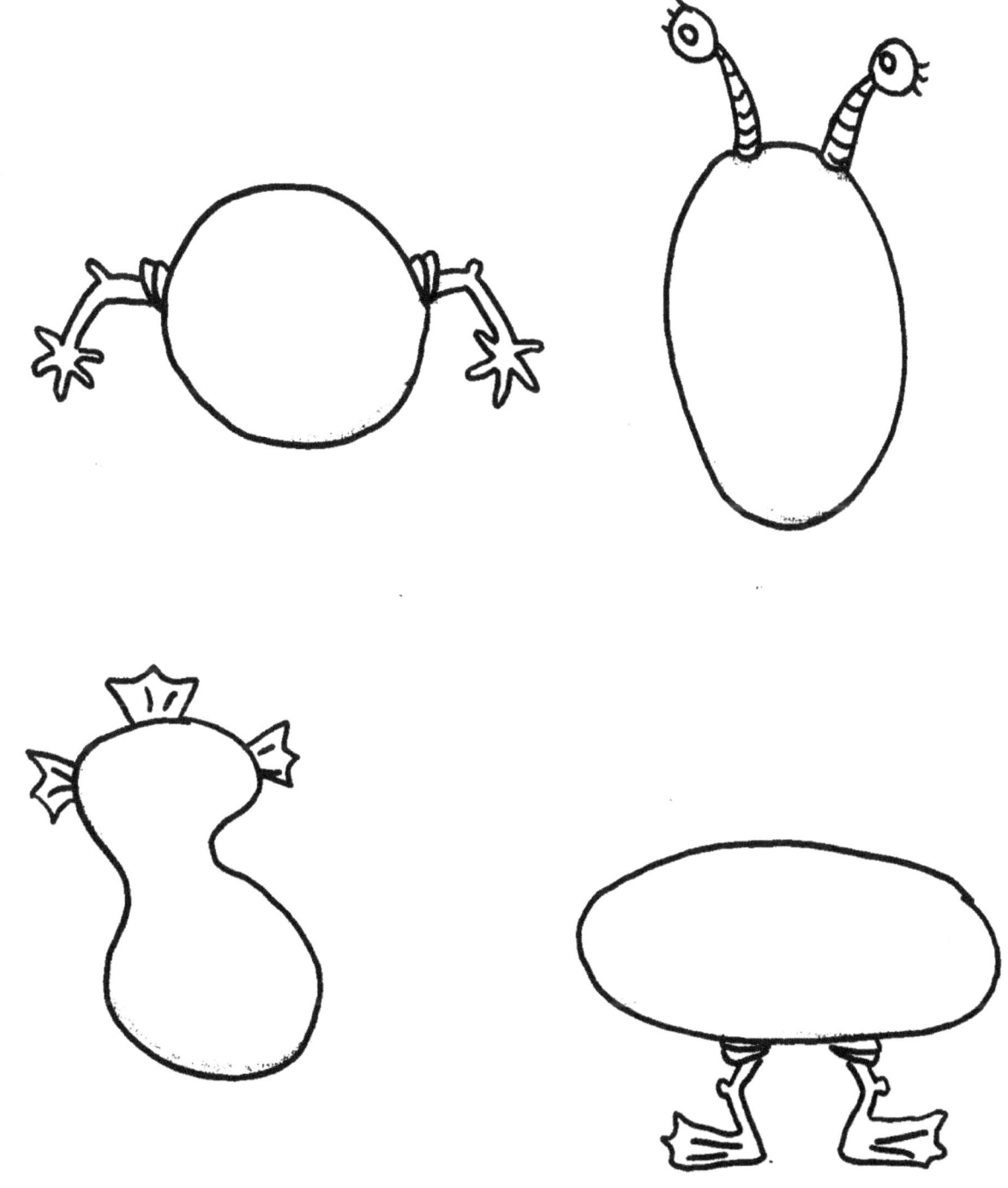

THIS ONE IS A UNICORN.

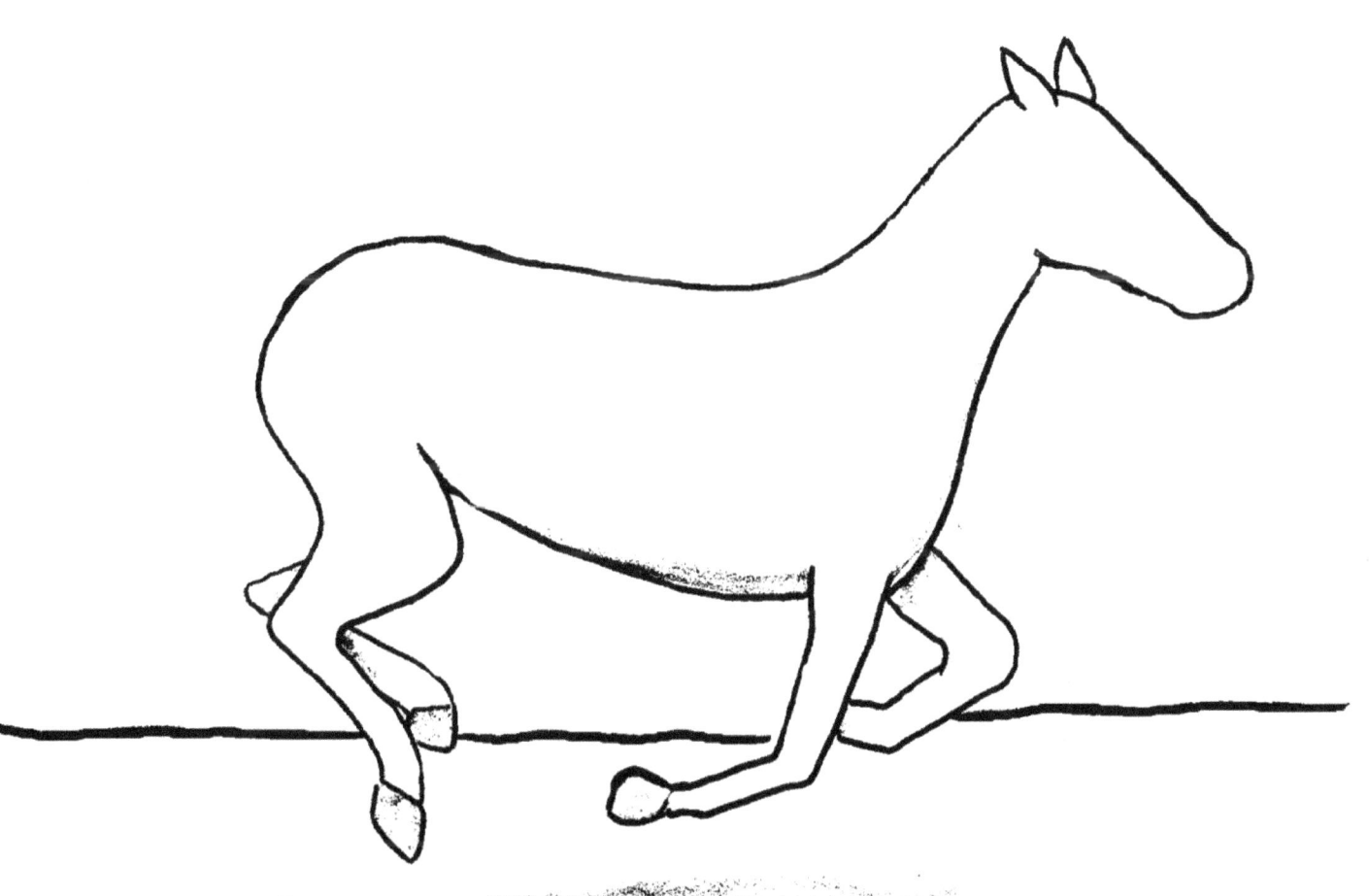

IS IT A FISH... OR SOMETHING ELSE?

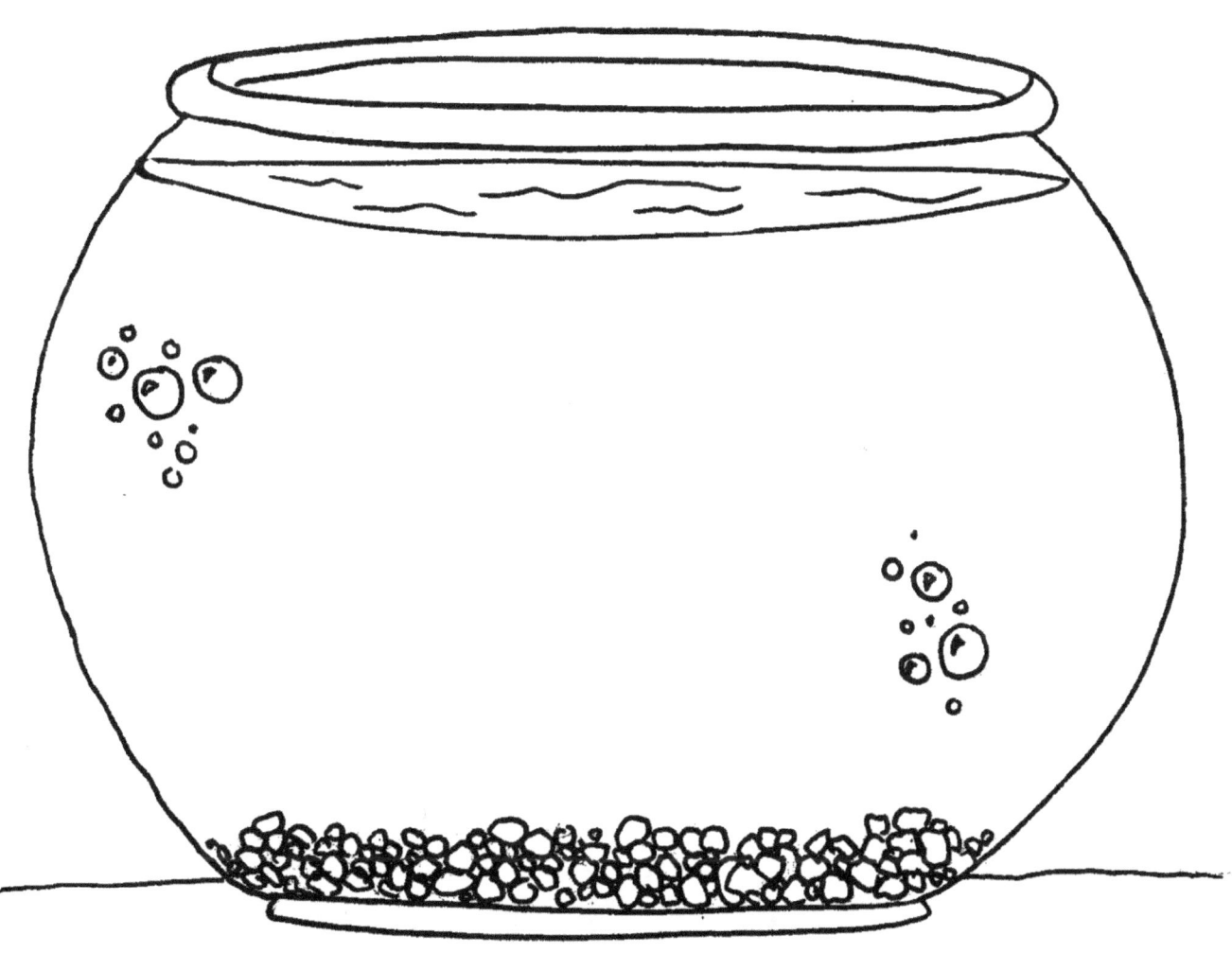

IT'S A PHOTO OF YOUR LONG-LOST COUSIN!

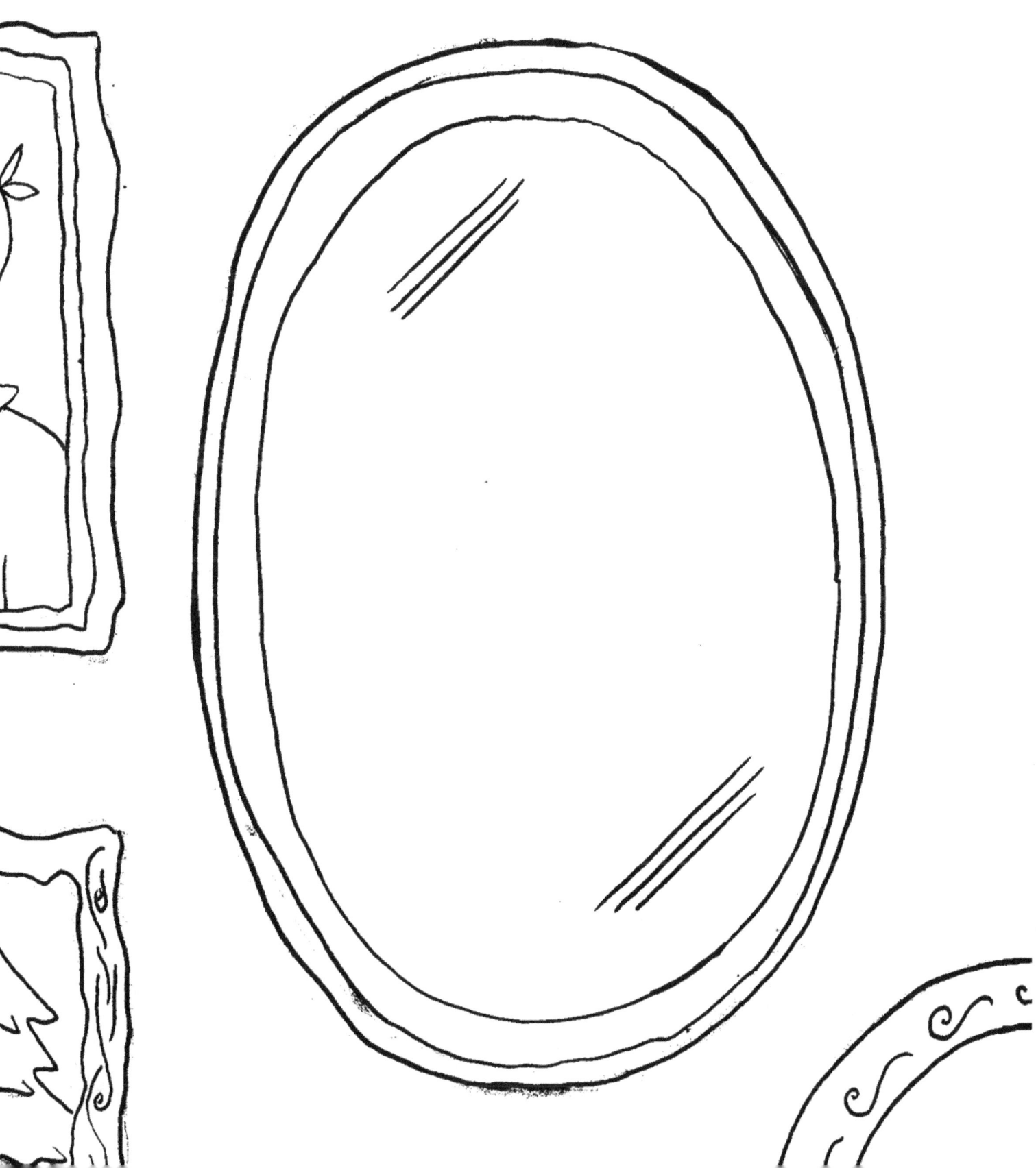

IS THAT A DOG ON A SURFBOARD?!

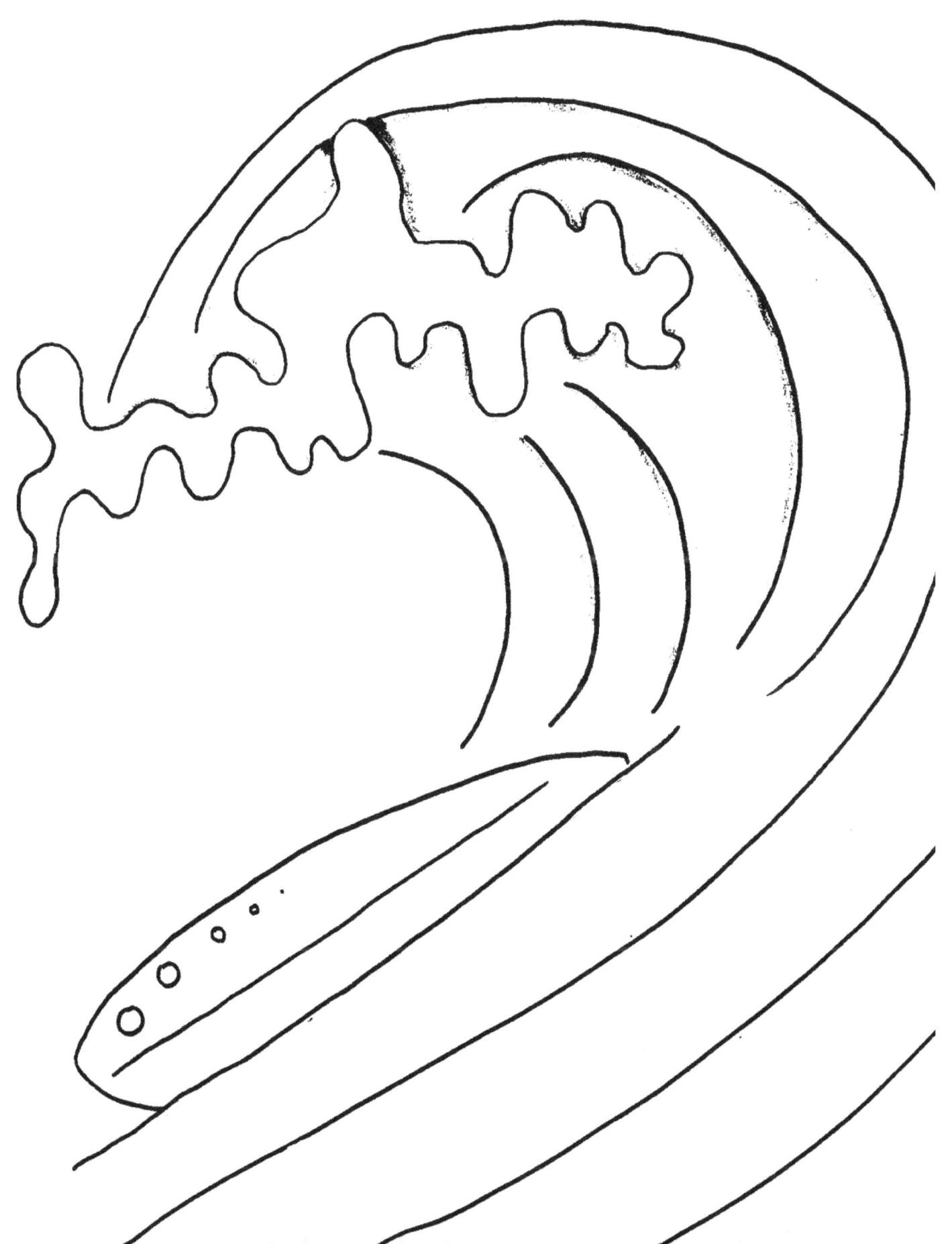

ADD SOME DISGUSTING TOPPINGS!

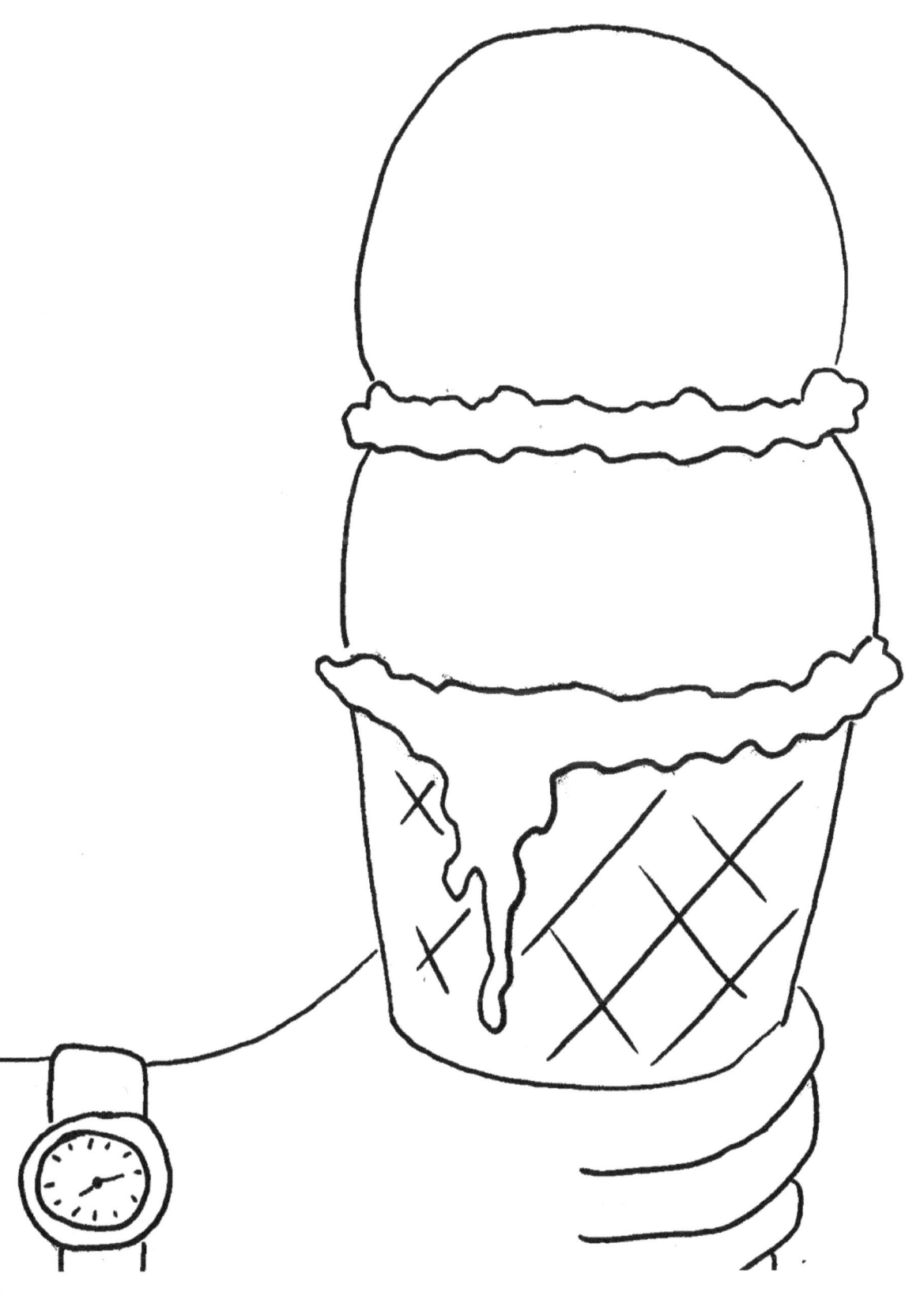

CAN YOU COPY THE DRAWINGS?

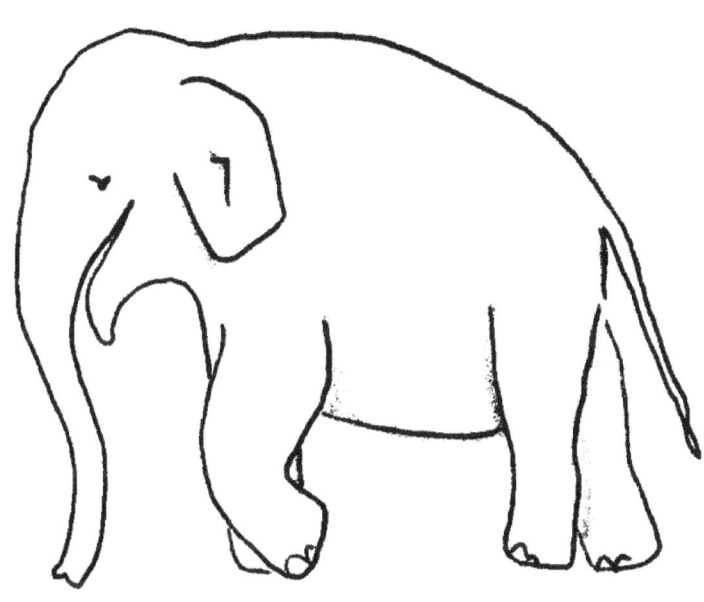

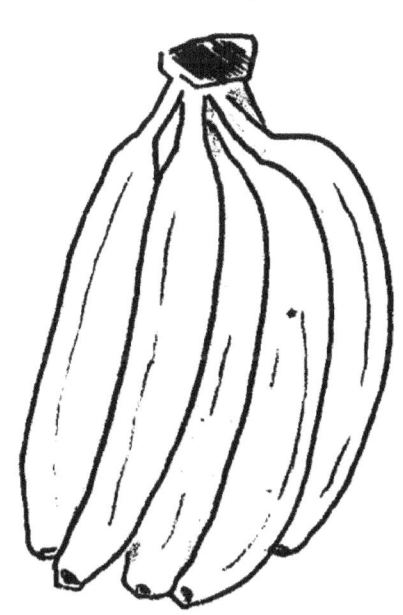

WHY DID THEY EAT THAT? THAT'S NOT FOOD!

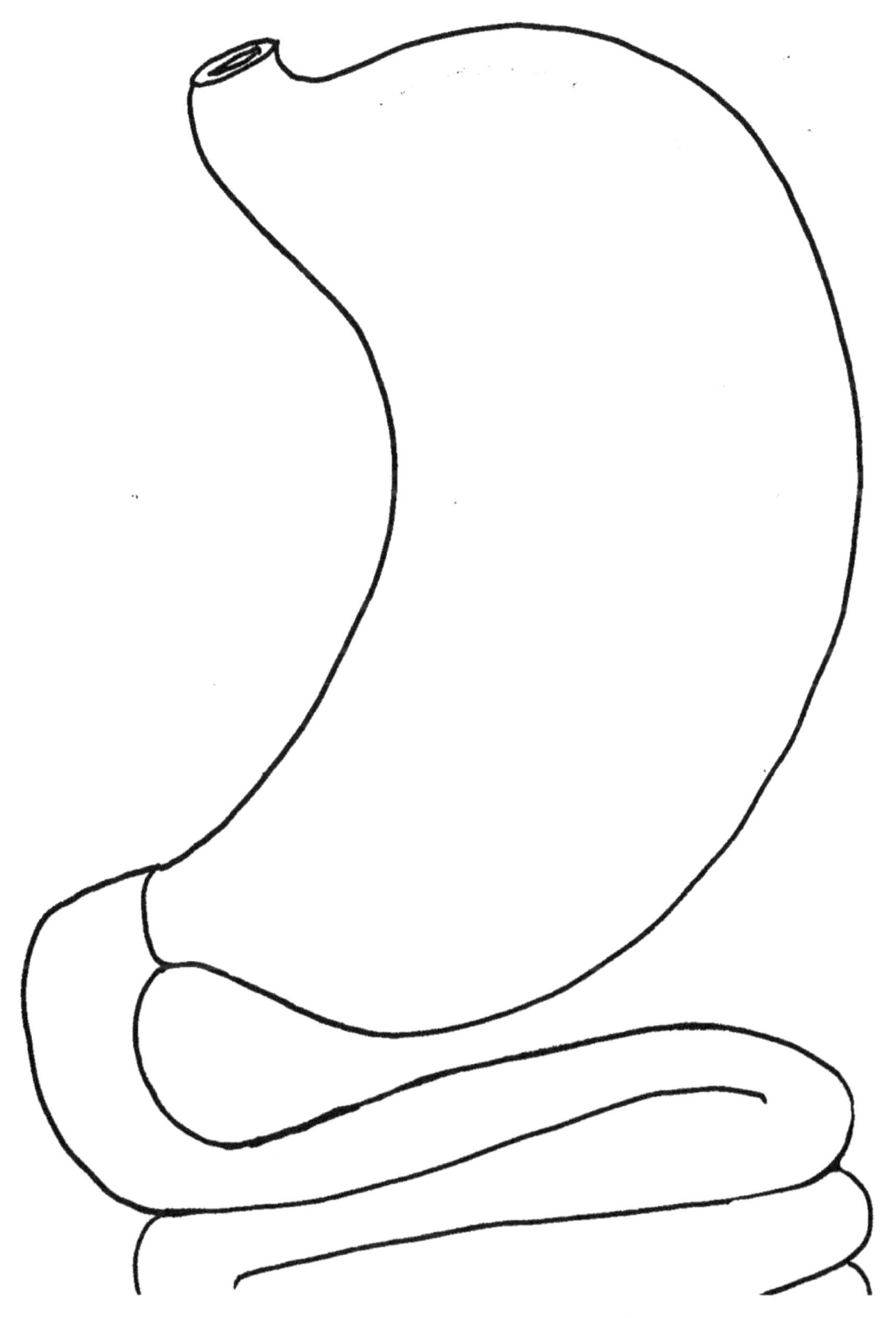

INVENT YOUR OWN SPACESHIP.

WHO HAS THE SEA SERPENT CAPTURED?

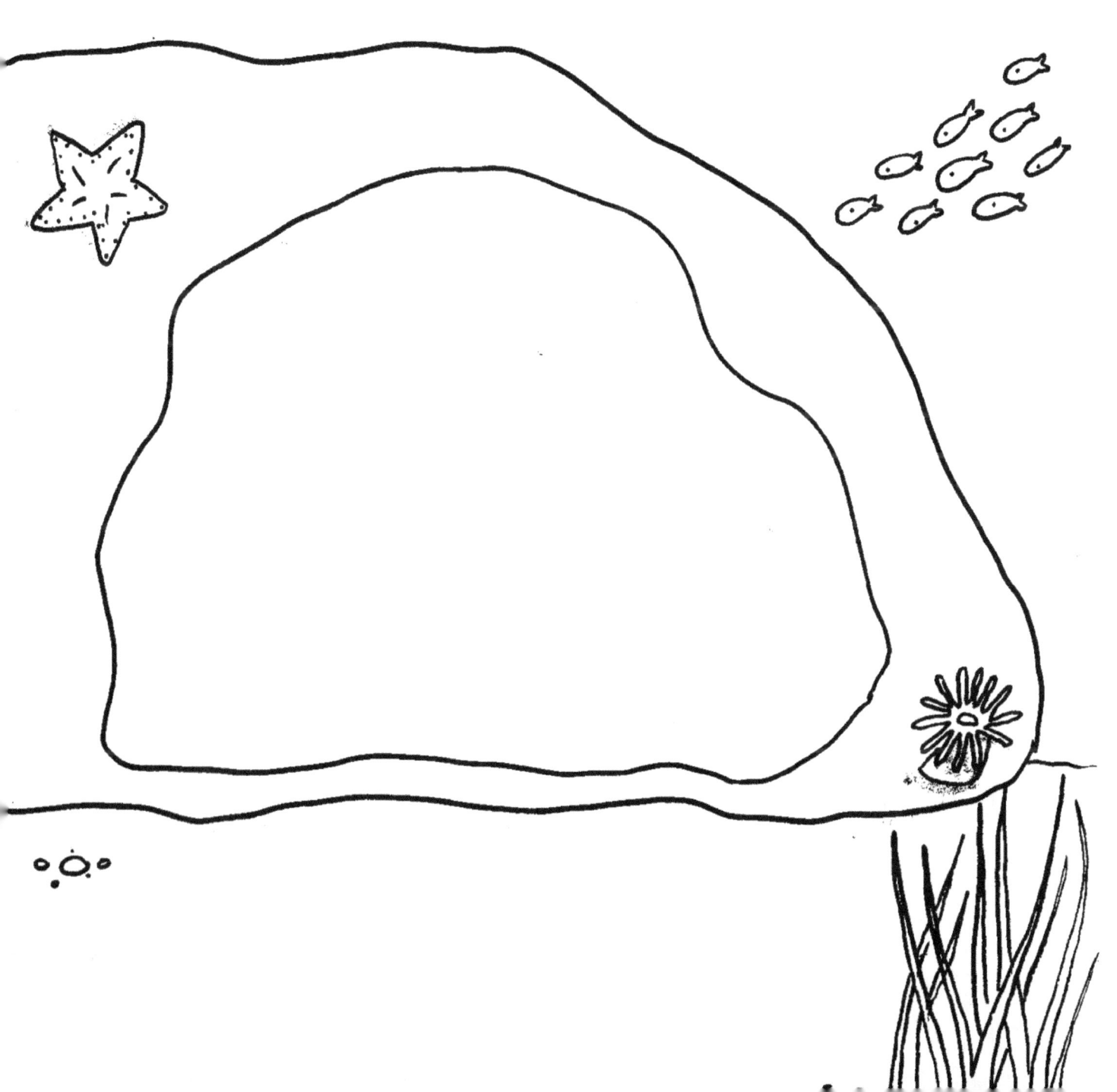

www.ingramcontent.com/pod-product-compliance
Lightning Source LLC
Chambersburg PA
CBHW080847220526
45467CB00008B/2415